AF593463

Divine Encounter

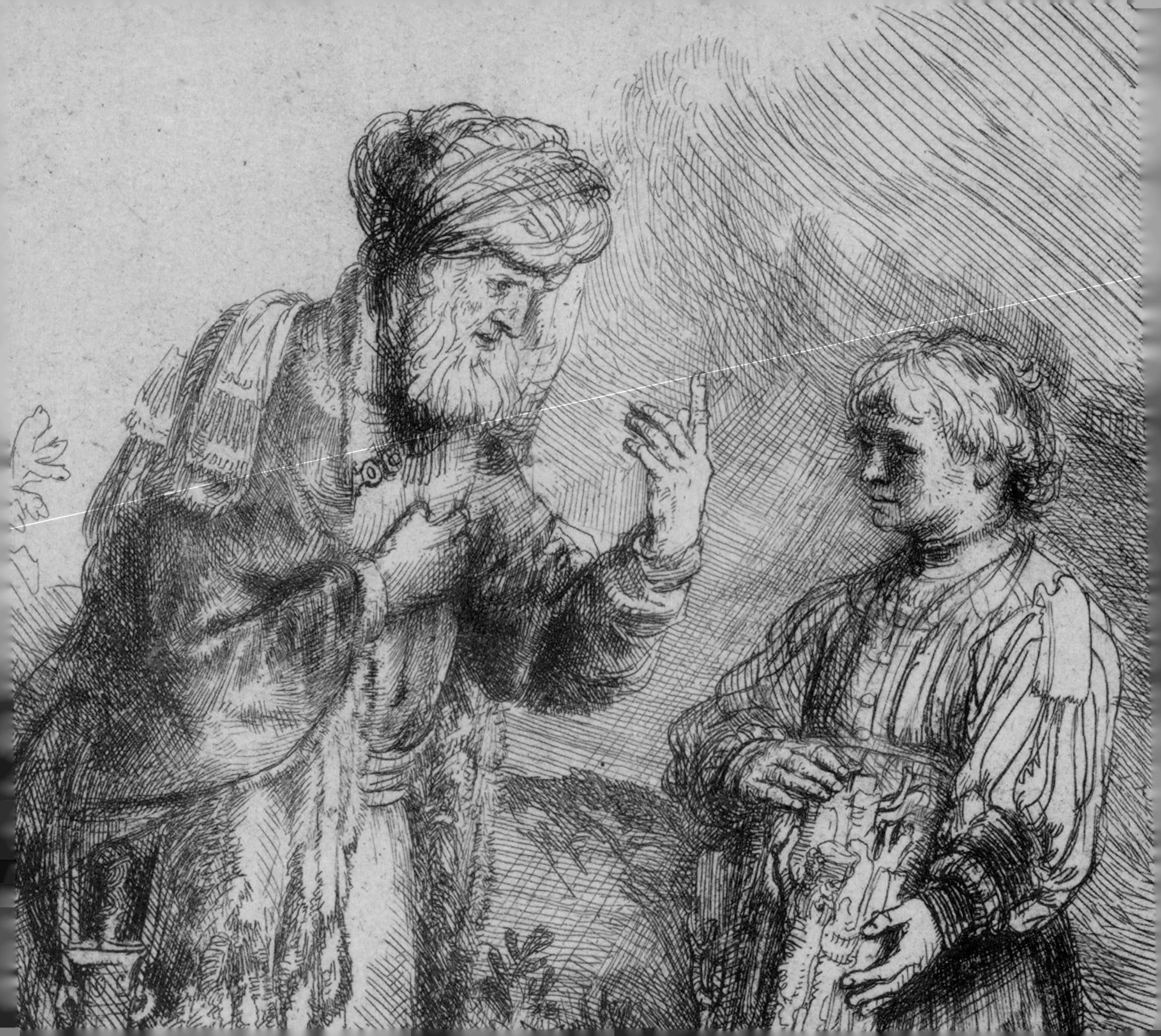

Divine Encounter

Rembrandt's Abraham and the Angels

Joanna Sheers Seidenstein

The Frick Collection, New York
in association with D Giles Limited, London

g

This book is published in conjunction with the exhibition *Divine Encounter: Rembrandt's Abraham and the Angels*, organized by The Frick Collection and on view from May 30 to August 20, 2017. Major funding for the exhibition is provided by the Isabel and Alfred Bader Fund, a Bader Philanthropy; the David Berg Foundation; and The Andrew W. Mellon Foundation. Additional support is generously provided by Otto Naumann Ltd., the Embassy of the Kingdom of the Netherlands, and the Netherland-America Foundation.

Published by The Frick Collection
Michaelyn Mitchell, Editor in Chief
Hilary Becker, Assistant Editor

In association with D Giles Limited

Copyedited and proofread by Rosanna Lewis
Designed by Alfonso Iacurci
Typeset in Caslon
Printed and bound in China

The Frick Collection
1 East 70th Street
New York, NY 10021
www.frick.org

D Giles Limited
4 Crescent Stables
139 Upper Richmond Road
London SW15 2TN
www.gilesltd.com

Front cover: Detail of *Abraham Entertaining the Angels*, 1646 (cat. 1)
Back cover and facing page: Details of *Abraham Entertaining the Angels*, 1656 (cat. 2)
Frontispiece: Detail of *Abraham and Isaac*, 1645 (cat. 4)
Page 6: Detail of *Abraham Caressing Isaac*, ca. 1637–45 (cat. 5)
Page 10: Detail of *Sacrifice of Isaac*, 1655 (cat. 7)

First printing

Photo Credits
© Christie's Images Limited 2012: fig. 19 • © Erich Lessing / Art Resource, NY: fig. 10 • Herbert Boswank: cat. 6 • © National Gallery, London / Art Resource, NY: fig. 26 • Photo courtesy The Metropolitan Museum of Art: cat. 1 • Studio Tromp, Rotterdam: fig. 22 • © The State Hermitage Museum / photo Vladimir Terebenin: figs. 1, 7, 20 • © Trustees of the British Museum: figs. 12, 23, 24 • © Scala / Art Resource, NY: fig. 4 • © Schloss Schönbrunn Kultur- und Betriebsges.m.b.H. / Digitalisat: Salon Iris: fig. 11

Library of Congress Cataloging-in-Publication Data
Names: Seidenstein, Joanna Sheers, author. | Rembrandt Harmenszoon van Rijn, 1606-1669. Paintings. Selections. | Frick Collection, host institution, issuing body.
Title: Divine encounter : Rembrandt's Abraham and the angels / Joanna Sheers Seidenstein.
Description: New York : The Frick Collection in association with D Giles Limited, London, [2017] | Published in conjunction with the exhibition "Divine Encounter: Rembrandt's Abraham and the Angels," organized by The Frick Collection and on view from May 30, 2017 to August 20, 2017. | Includes bibliographical references.
Identifiers: LCCN 2016044721 | ISBN 9781911282037
Subjects: LCSH: Rembrandt Harmenszoon van Rijn, 1606-1669. Abraham entertaining the angels--Exhibitions.
Classification: LCC ND653.R4 A62 2017 | DDC 759.9492--dc23
LC record available at https://lccn.loc.gov/2016044721

ISBN: 978-1-911282-03-7

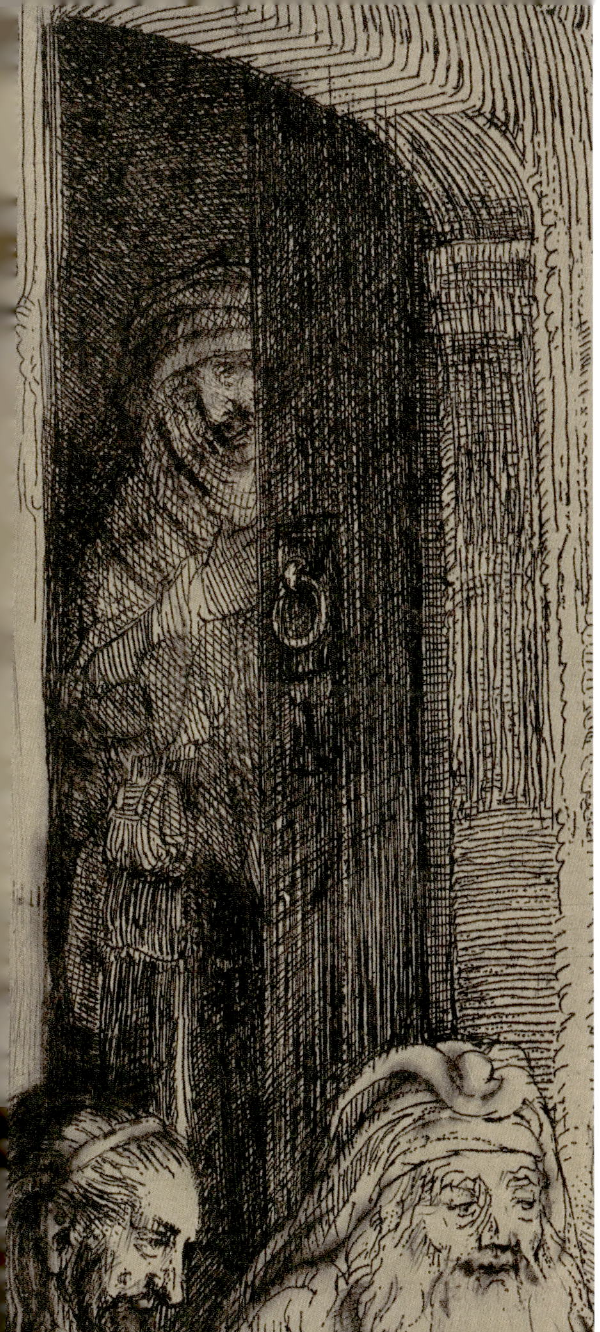

Contents

Foreword 6

Acknowledgments 8

Rembrandt and the Unseen: Perception and Revelation in the Abraham Narrative 11

Bibliography 65

Index 71

Foreword

In 1646, on a tiny panel fewer than nine inches wide, Rembrandt van Rijn (1606–1669) produced one of his most captivating images: a scene of breathtaking calm at the heart of which sits a winged creature ablaze with light. Traceable to 1647, when an Amsterdam merchant, a Martin van den Broeck, traded a collection of diamonds, silverwork, and paintings, including an "Abraham with the three angels by Rembrandt," to Andries Ackersloot in exchange for a supply of ropes, masts, and iron, the picture has passed through the collections of a number of notable figures: Rembrandt's former pupil Ferdinand Bol, possibly the seventeenth-century Amsterdam burgomaster Jan Six, and, with the work in England by the early nineteenth century, the American expatriate painter Benjamin West. It has remained in private hands and has been publicly exhibited only a handful of times over the years. Among Rembrandt's lesser-known masterpieces, this extraordinary painting is the inspiration for the exhibition this publication accompanies. This tightly focused show takes as its subject Rembrandt's depictions of Abraham, the first of the Old Testament patriarchs, whose various

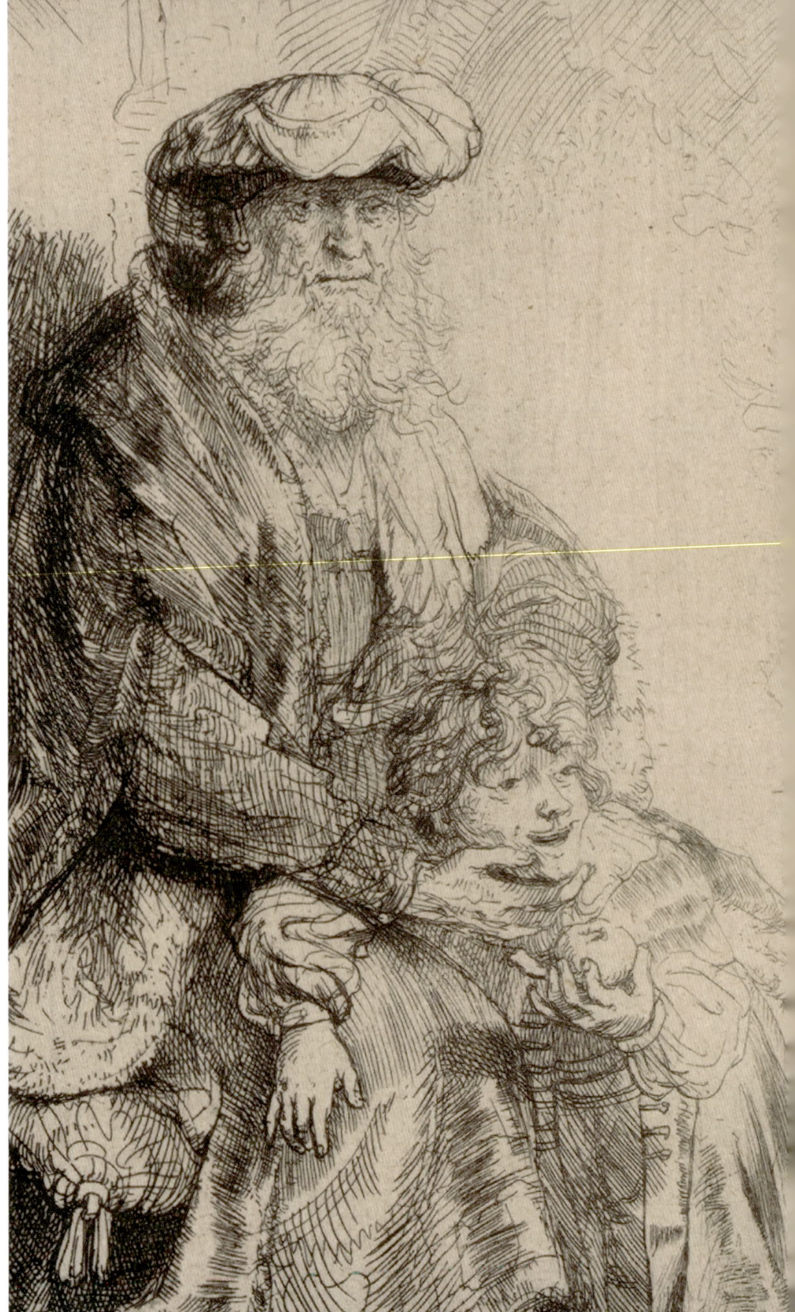

encounters with the divine offered the artist a range of fascinating pictorial challenges. In the 1646 painting and in the other works in the show—a selection of prints and drawings ranging in date from the late 1630s to the end of the 1650s—Rembrandt explored different possibilities for the representation of divine presence and revelation, raising questions of artistic, theological, and philosophical significance.

I would like to acknowledge the many members of my staff who contributed to this project, first and foremost Joanna Sheers Seidenstein, Anne L. Poulet Curatorial Fellow, who proposed and organized the exhibition, and Xavier F. Salomon, Peter Jay Sharp Chief Curator, whose guidance and efforts were essential to its success. Michaelyn Mitchell, Editor in Chief, oversaw the production of the publication and, together with Assistant Editor Hilary Becker, edited the text. I am most grateful to them and to our publishing partner, D Giles Limited, for producing this beautiful book. For various other aspects of the project, thanks are due to Adrian Anderson, Michael Bodycomb, Rebecca Brooke, Rika Burnham, Tia Chapman, Diane Farynyk, Allison Galea, Vivian Gill, Lisa Goble, Joseph Godla, Robert Goldsmith, Caitlin Henningsen, Anita Jorgensen, Patrick King, Adrienne Lei, Genevra Le Voci, Alexis Light, Alison Lonshein, David Martin, Michael Paccione, Heidi Rosenau, Stephen Saitas, Jeannette Sharpless, Joseph Shatoff, Floyd Sweeting, and Sean Troxell.

It is a pleasure to thank the lenders to the exhibition. Our deep appreciation goes to the private collector who generously agreed to part with Rembrandt's 1646 *Abraham Entertaining the Angels* for the run of the show, as well as to the National Gallery of Art in Washington, D.C., the Metropolitan Museum of Art, the Kupferstichkabinett of the Staatliche Kunstsammlungen Dresden, the Morgan Library & Museum, and all our colleagues at those institutions.

For their generous support of this exhibition and publication, we are profoundly grateful to the Isabel and Alfred Bader Fund, the David Berg Foundation, and The Andrew W. Mellon Foundation, as well as to Otto Naumann Ltd., the Embassy of the Kingdom of the Netherlands, and the Netherland-America Foundation.

Ian Wardropper
Director, The Frick Collection

Acknowledgments

It is a pleasure to express my gratitude to the many people who made this publication and the exhibition it accompanies possible. My warmest thanks go to Ian Wardropper, Director of The Frick Collection, for his faith in and support of the project, and to Xavier F. Salomon, Peter Jay Sharp Chief Curator, for his invaluable direction and advice at every stage. Working with Xavier has been a great privilege, and I owe him my endless appreciation and admiration. I am also immensely grateful to Susan Grace Galassi, Senior Curator, whose mentorship I have had the great fortune of enjoying for the past decade and a half and who has been a constant source of wisdom, encouragement, and kindness. To Xavier, Susan, and the other curators at the Frick, past and present— Denise Allen, Colin B. Bailey, Peggy Iacono, the late Edgar Munhall, Aimee Ng, and Charlotte Vignon—I offer heartfelt thanks for their support and inspiring examples.

I echo Ian Wardropper's thanks to our funders and lenders for their exceptional generosity. My deepest gratitude goes to the anonymous lender of Rembrandt's 1646 *Abraham Entertaining the Angels* for this extraordinary loan. I also extend my thanks to Andrew Robison, Jonathan Bober, Meg Grasselli, and Gregory Jecmen at the National Gallery of Art in Washington, D.C.; Nadine Orenstein at the Metropolitan Museum of Art; Stephanie Buck of the Kupferstichkabinett of the Staatliche Kunstsammlungen Dresden; and Colin B. Bailey, John Marciari, and Ilona van Tuinen at the Morgan Library & Museum. Without the generosity and collegiality of these individuals, which they demonstrated in myriad ways, this project would not have been possible.

Many other colleagues spoke with me about the project and shared their expertise and advice, among them George Bisacca, Monique Blanc, Hugo Chapman, Navina Najat Haidar, Elfriede Iby, Ebba Koch, Susan Kuretsky, Jan Leja, Otto Naumann, Esmée Quodbach, Bill Robinson, Pieter Roelofs, Peter Schatborn, Stephanie Schrader, Michael Wohlfahrt, Louise Wood Ruby, and Michael Zell. Larry Silver has been especially generous with his time and guidance. I am also indebted to Professors Silver and Zell and to Shelley Perlove and Thomas Ketelsen, whose work on Rembrandt's depictions of Abraham has been of fundamental importance for the present study. Jacquelyn Coutré, whom I am lucky to count as a friend, offered invaluable feedback on my essay, and meaningful support.

At the Frick, I have been privileged to work with an extraordinary group of people whose contributions are too numerous and too significant to recount in their entirety. I am grateful to Robert Goldsmith, Joe Shatoff, Mike Paccione, and Alison Lonshein for their essential support and to Tia Chapman, David Martin, Genevra Le Voci, and everyone in the External

Affairs Department whose work made this project a reality. I owe deep appreciation to the media relations team headed by Heidi Rosenau, with special thanks to Alexis Light for brilliantly managing the publicity for this project. For bringing the exhibition to fruition with their usual finesse and for invaluable guidance along the way, I thank everyone in the Registrar and Conservation Departments: Diane Farynyk, Allison Galea, Jeannette Sharpless, Joe Godla, Julia Day, Brittany Luberda, Gianna Puzzo, Patrick King, and Adrian Anderson. The beauty of the installation is the result of the expertise and efforts of exhibition designer Stephen Saitas and lighting designer Anita Jorgensen. I am immensely grateful to Editor in Chief Michaelyn Mitchell for her management of this publication and for the great care and patience with which she, Assistant Editor Hilary Becker, and editorial volunteer Serena Rattazzi refined the text. It was also a pleasure to work with our publishing partner Dan Giles. Jenna Nugent, who coordinates the Poulet fellowship program, among so many other things, has been a continual source of information and kindness. My thanks also go to Rika Burnham, Caitlin Henningsen, Adrienne Lei, and the entire Education Department for the programming they have organized; to Michael Bodycomb, Rebecca Brooke, Vivian Gill, Lisa Goble, Floyd Sweeting, and Sean Troxell for their significant contributions; and to the Frick's archivists and the staff of the Frick Art Reference Library for all they have done to support my research. I am especially grateful to Aaron Wile and Eloise Owens for their feedback on my essay. I also thank them, along with Caitlin Henningsen, Adam Eaker, and Emma Capron, for their advice and wonderful company. Finally, my heartfelt gratitude goes to former curatorial intern Yasmine El Gheur, who offered excellent assistance in the spring of 2016, and to Charlotte Rulkens, former Ayesha Bulchandani Curatorial Intern, with whom I had the pleasure of working in the fall of 2015. Charlotte's superb and stimulating research and countless other efforts were essential to the success of this project.

My interest in Rembrandt's work developed over the course of my doctoral studies at the Institute of Fine Arts of New York University, where, from 2009 to 2014, I held the Kaplan-Fisch Fellowship for the Connoisseurship of European Painting. For this funding and the extraordinary training and opportunities it made possible, I am deeply grateful to Mark Fisch and Thomas Kaplan and to the institute's faculty and administration, particularly Jonathan Brown and former director Mariët Westermann, who has been a most supportive and inspiring adviser and mentor.

Finally, I thank my grandparents, Joseph and Lillian Mordas, and the late Harriet M. Sheers, my parents, James and Deborah Sheers, my mother-in-law, Susan Seidenstein, my husband, Marc Seidenstein, and the rest of my family for their love and support. With gratitude and admiration, I dedicate this publication to my parents.

Joanna Sheers Seidenstein

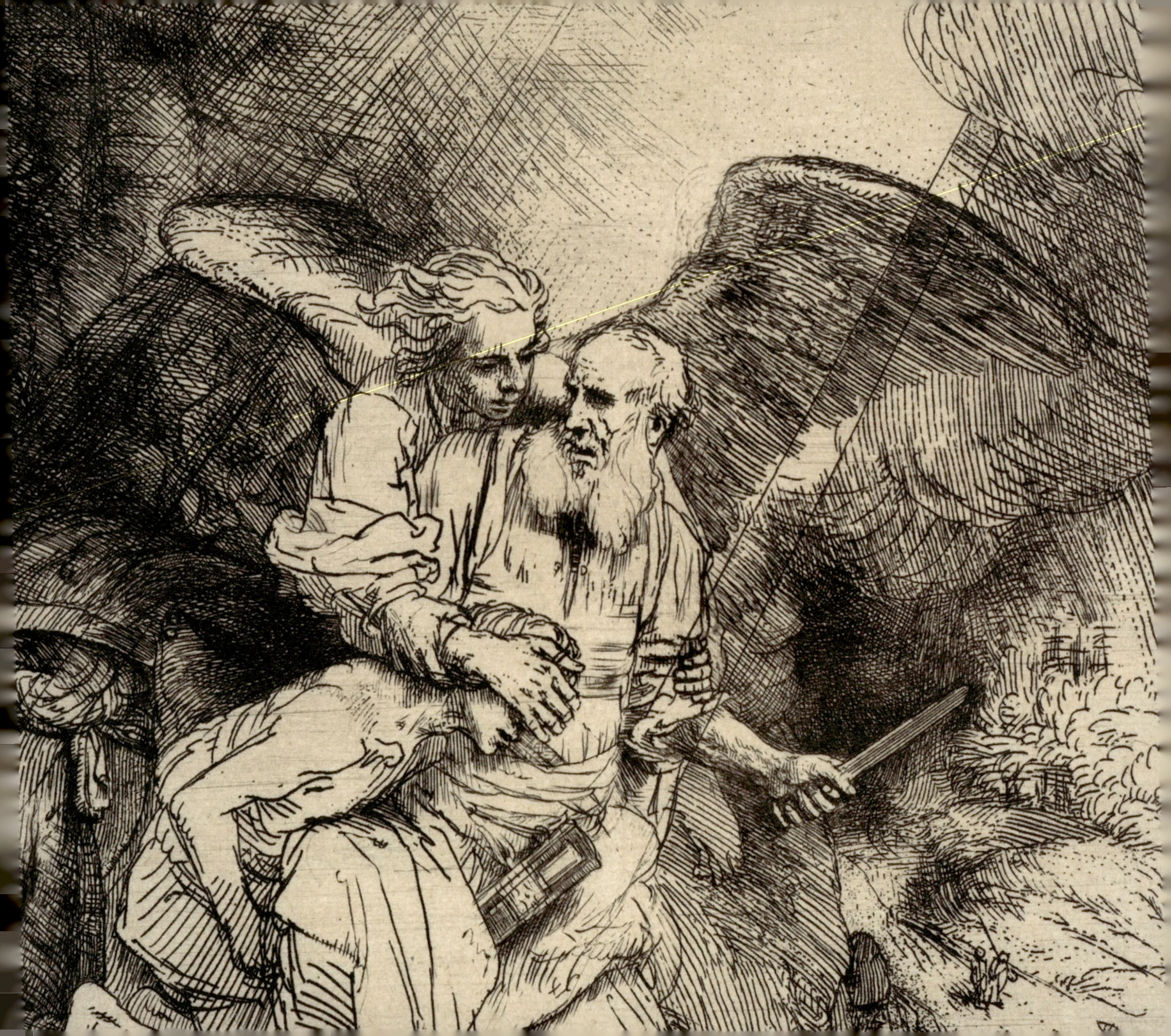

Rembrandt and the Unseen

Perception and Revelation in the Abraham Narrative

Chapter 18 of Genesis begins with the explicit statement that the Lord *appeared* to Abraham (in the Hebrew, *vayerá*, literally "was seen by" him). Immediately following this verse is an enigmatic account relating the visit of three travelers to whom Abraham offers food, water, and rest. While eating, the guests ask about Abraham's aged wife, Sarah, and one of them announces that she will give birth to a son in a year's time. Hearing this, Sarah laughs in disbelief, prompting the speaker—now identified in the text as God himself—to chastise her, asking, "Is anything too great for the Lord?" He thus reveals to Abraham and Sarah the divine and providential nature of this visitation. What we are to understand about what the couple *saw*, however, is not readily evident. Rembrandt treated this episode on two occasions: in a tiny painted panel of 1646 (cat. 1) and in an etching made ten years later (cat. 2). In these works, both known as *Abraham Entertaining the Angels*, the artist grapples, in strikingly different ways, with the nature of this divine encounter and the complexities of its representation in pictorial form.

This painting and etching are two of several works in which Rembrandt treated episodes from the life of Abraham. In the Judeo-Christian tradition, Abraham is the progenitor of the Jewish people, the individual with whom God makes his everlasting covenant, promising descendants as numerous as the stars in the sky. The patriarch's story unfolds over the course of several chapters in Genesis, the first book of the Hebrew Bible, or Old Testament, and is replete with encounters with the divine, among them, the Lord's command to Abraham to settle in Canaan; the establishment of the covenant; the foretelling of the birth of his and Sarah's son, Isaac; the call to banish Abraham's firstborn, Ishmael; and the subsequent command to sacrifice Isaac on Mount Moriah. In some instances, the Lord only speaks to Abraham; in another, the "word of God" comes to him "in a vision"; in yet others, *malachim* (messengers, or angels) speak to or approach the patriarch; and in three episodes, including Genesis 18, the Lord himself appears to him. The Abraham narrative held a place of central importance in the predominantly Calvinist society of the Dutch Republic, foremost as the story of a covenant that, according to Calvin, was one and the same with Christ's promise to all mankind.[1] Rembrandt's imagery often relates

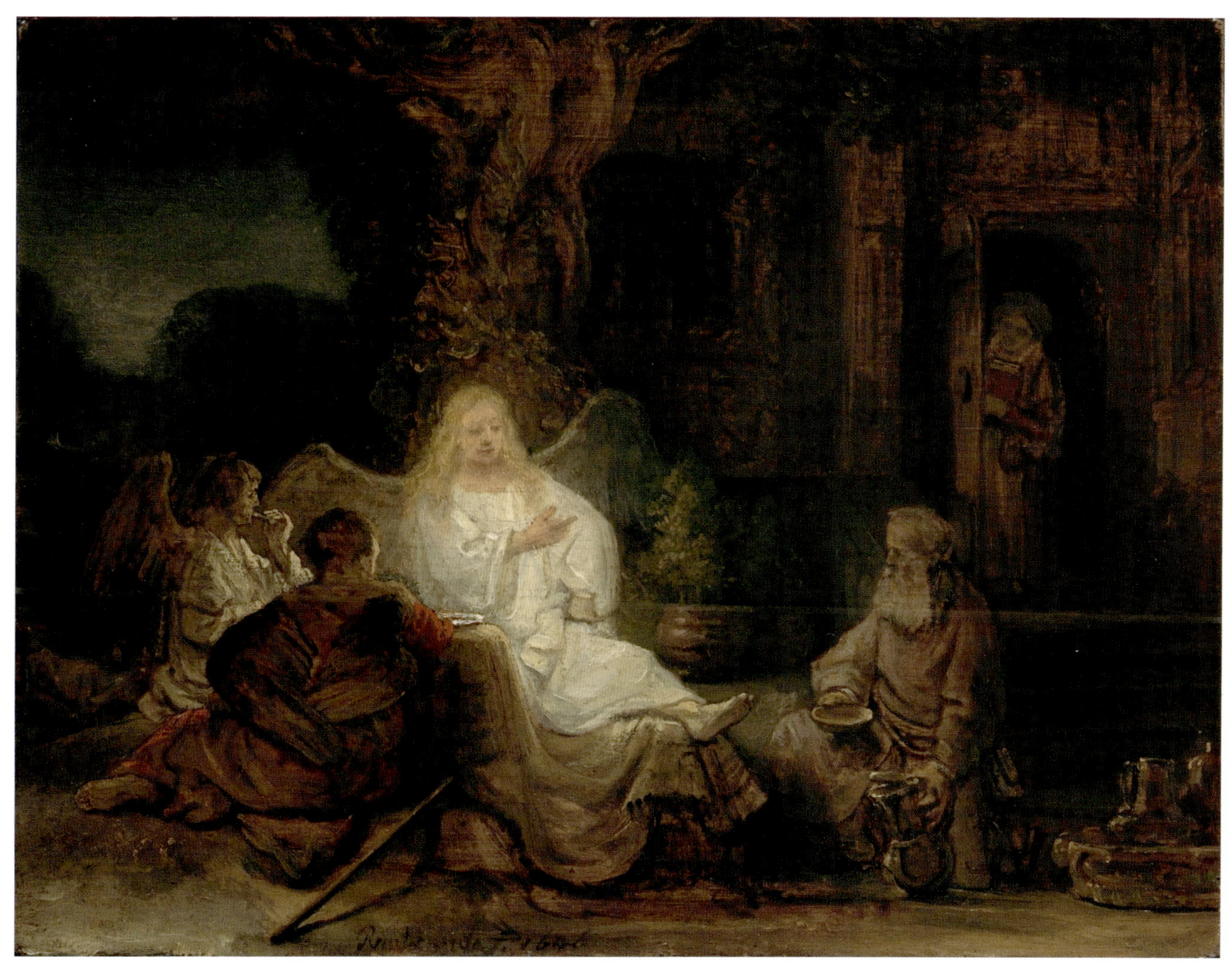

Cat. 1

Rembrandt, *Abraham Entertaining the Angels*, 1646
Oil on oak panel
6 ⅜ × 8 ⅜ inches (16.1 × 21.1 cm)
Private collection

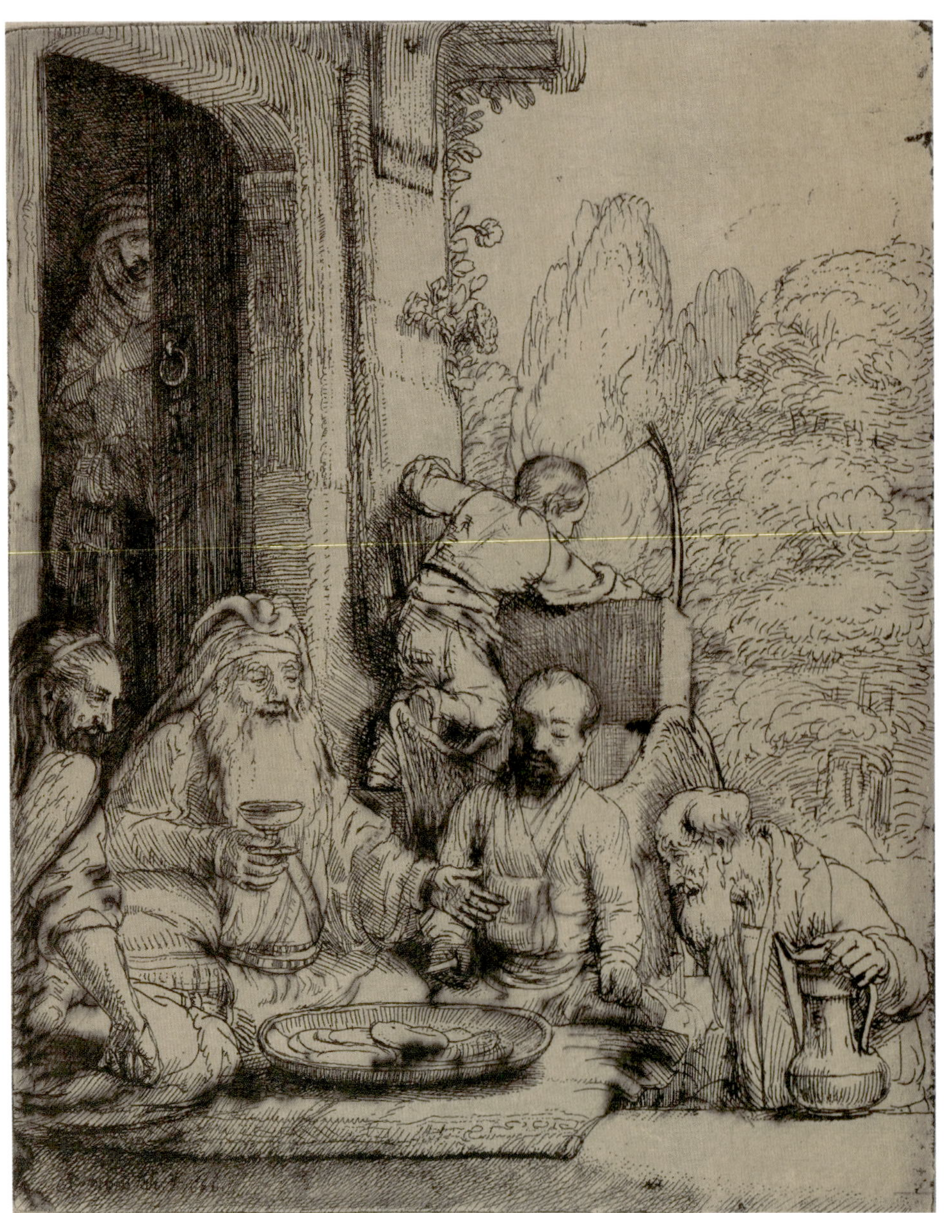

Cat. 2

Rembrandt, *Abraham Entertaining the Angels*, 1656
Etching and drypoint on Japanese paper, only state
6 5⁄16 × 5 1⁄8 inches (16.1 × 13 cm)
National Gallery of Art, Washington; New Century Fund

specifically to Calvinist exegesis.[2] At the same time, the artist was highly receptive to other sources and stimuli—the largely Catholic pictorial tradition he had inherited and the cosmopolitan culture of seventeenth-century Amsterdam, among others. Ultimately, his interests were as much intellectual as they were spiritual. Viewing Calvinism's prohibition of anthropomorphic representations of God less as a mandate and more as a fascinating artistic challenge, he continually devised new means to convey divine presence. Rembrandt's depictions of Genesis 18, along with his other images of the patriarch, demonstrate the artist's evolving understanding of the relationship between sight and faith and of the nature of revelation. With these works, he raised major questions about the divine and human perception thereof.

ACTION/REACTION

Encounters between mortals and immortals, drawn from both Judeo-Christian and Greco-Roman sources, were long-favored subjects in European art. Their encapsulation of a story into a single, pivotal moment, usually involving some reversal of fortune, made them ideal for independent easel paintings. As Albert Blankert observed, such reversals, wherein one emotional state gives way to another, appealed enormously to Rembrandt, who early in his career mastered the depiction of fleeting motion and emotion, as, for example, in his *Sacrifice of Isaac* of 1635 (fig. 1).[3] This monumental work, the artist's first painting of a scene from the Abraham narrative, treats the episode from Genesis 22 in which the patriarch, obeying God's command, proceeds to take his son Isaac's life but is stopped at the last moment by a messenger of the Lord. Although the text of Genesis describes the messenger only as "calling out" to Abraham, artists had long depicted the scene as a physical, and visual, encounter. Rembrandt follows this pictorial tradition, showing a winged angel grasping the patriarch's wrist. Even more than his predecessors, he seeks to capture the instantaneity with which Abraham sees and reacts to this intervention. Looking directly at the youthful angel, behind whose wings the sky breaks open with divine light, Abraham expresses both surprise and understanding. His mouth falls open and his eyes fill with tears, his sorrow turning to relief. Most remarkably, his hand is shown releasing the knife, which appears in mid-air. It was in regard to another painting, *The Resurrection of Christ* (Alte Pinakothek, Munich), in which a sword similarly slips from a startled soldier's hand and tumbles through the air, that Rembrandt articulated, in 1639, his sole documented comment about art making: his aim to observe "the most natural motions."[4] In that work, as in the *Sacrifice of Isaac*, the sight of the miraculous yields an immediate reaction discernible in the motions of both body and mind. As we will see, however, Rembrandt's understanding of "the most natural motions" would change over time.

Fig. 1 Rembrandt, *Sacrifice of Isaac*, 1635. Oil on canvas, 75 15⁄16 × 51 15⁄16 inches (193 × 132 cm). State Hermitage Museum, St. Petersburg

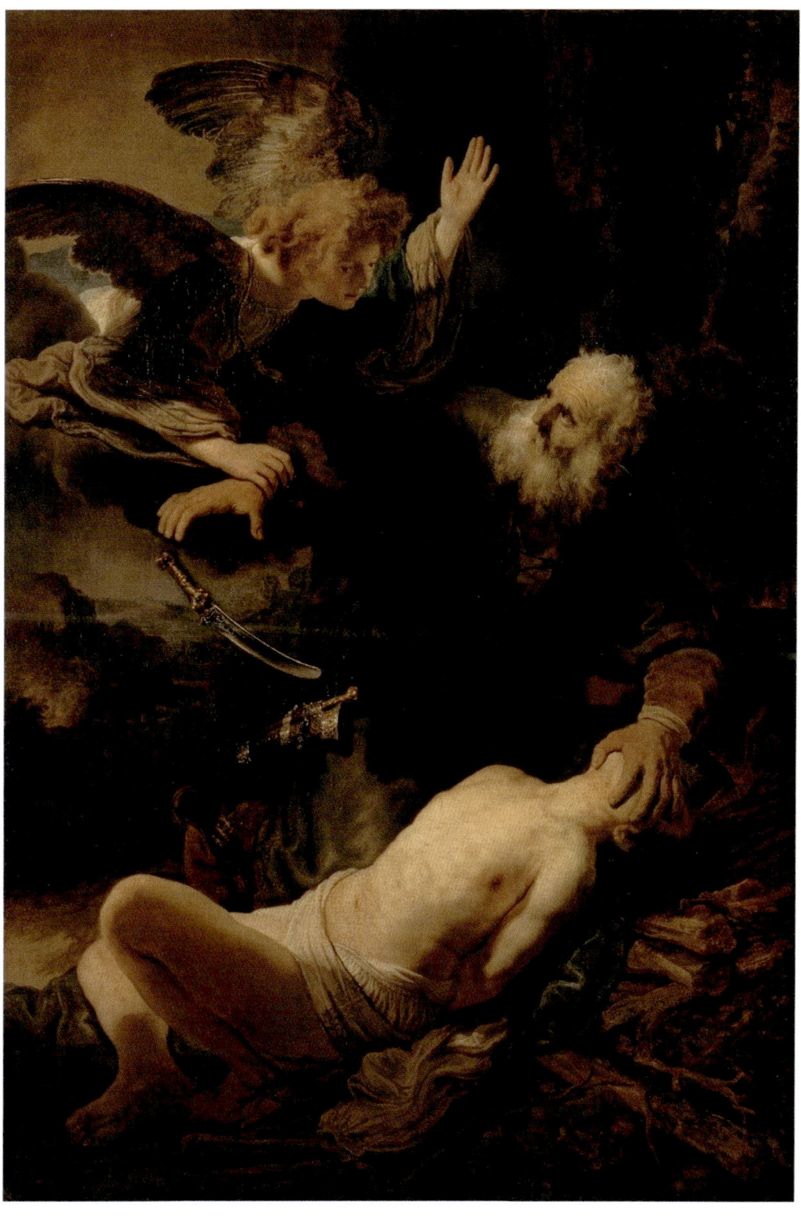

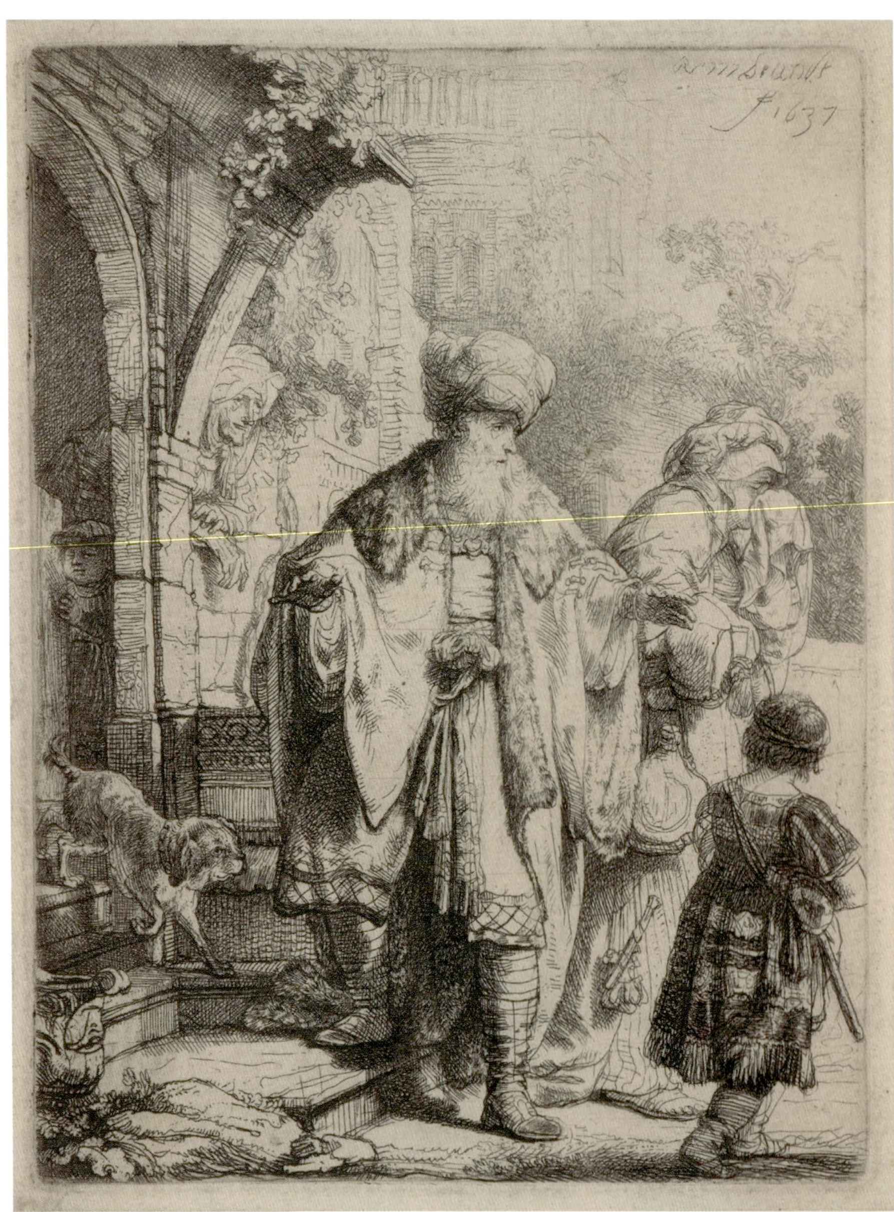

Cat. 3

Rembrandt, *Abraham Casting Out Hagar and Ishmael*, 1637
Etching with touches of drypoint, only state,
4 ⅞ × 3 ¾ inches (12.5 × 9.5 cm)
The Morgan Library & Museum, New York (RvR 38)

SUSPENSION AND ANTICIPATION

Over the course of the decade following his masterpiece of 1635, Rembrandt made three etchings depicting other scenes from the Abraham narrative. In these prints, the artist developed a new approach to biblical imagery, taking into account the story in its entirety and incorporating into each scene reminiscences of the past and anticipations of the future. As Shelley Perlove and Larry Silver have discussed, his method mirrored the hermeneutics embodied in the Dutch States Bible.[5] First published in 1637, this government-sponsored translation from the original Hebrew and Greek contains numerous marginal annotations, offering detailed explanations of each biblical passage (largely based on Calvin's writings), often with cross-references to other parts of the Bible. Drawing from scripture, yet remaining sensitive to its tensions and ambiguities, Rembrandt offered his own interpretations and raised probing questions.

The first of his Abraham etchings, dated 1637, treats the episode from Genesis 21 in which Abraham expels from his home his firstborn son, Ishmael, and the boy's mother, Hagar (cat. 3). Earlier in Genesis, before the divine announcement about Isaac's birth, Sarah, unable to conceive, had persuaded Abraham to father a child with Hagar, their slave. Some time after Isaac's birth, Sarah sees Ishmael mocking her son. Concerned that he not share in Isaac's inheritance, she tells Abraham to cast Ishmael and his mother out of their home. Abraham is pained by this proposition, but God speaks to him and commands him to do as Sarah says, affirming his earlier promise that while Isaac will inherit his covenant, Ishmael will also become the father of a great nation.

The Dutch States Bible contains a note citing the apostle Paul's commentary on this episode in his epistle to the Galatians (4:21–31). There, associating Ishmael and Hagar with those who did not accept Christ as the Messiah, Paul refers to Ishmael's "persecution" of Isaac. He also contrasts Ishmael's birth "according to the flesh" with Isaac's miraculous conception and presents Hagar as mother of the Jews, bound by law, and Sarah, the free woman, as mother of the Christians, liberated from Jewish law by their faith in Christ. This reversal of Jewish tradition, which emphatically traces the lineage of the Jews to Abraham through Isaac, gave rise to a long tradition of negative, antisemitic portrayals of Hagar and Ishmael.[6] In the early sixteenth century, however, a significant shift in the visual tradition occurred, even though the Pauline interpretation of the biblical episode, which was embraced and promoted by Calvin in his *Institutes of the Christian Religion* of 1536, would persist into the seventeenth century.[7] Lucas van Leyden (1494–1533), for example, produced two prints in which he framed this banishment as a sorrowful farewell with a distinctly sympathetic Hagar and Ishmael. In one of these works (fig. 2), Abraham touches Hagar's sleeve tenderly, while the young Ishmael stands between his parents, looking up at his

Fig. 2 Lucas van Leyden (1494–1533), *Abraham Casting Out Hagar and Ishmael*, 1516. Engraving, 5 13⁄16 × 4 13⁄16 inches (14.8 × 12.3 cm). Rijksprentenkabinet, Rijksmuseum, Amsterdam

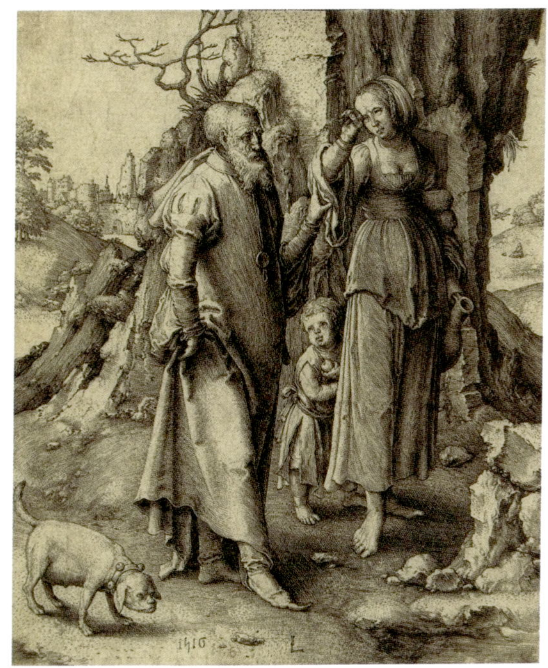

father and holding a small apple—perhaps his only nourishment for the journey ahead. With one hand, Hagar wipes tears from her face and with the other she holds a pitcher—the vessel that will, later in Genesis 21, run empty, leaving her and Ishmael wandering in the wilderness without water until an angel calls to the desperate woman and the Lord "opens her eyes" to a nearby well.[8]

Lucas's prints provided an important model for subsequent artists, among them Pieter Lastman (1583–1633), Rembrandt's teacher. Lastman produced a similarly sympathetic depiction in 1612 (Hamburg Kunsthalle), which his famous pupil copied in a drawing (Albertina, Vienna).[9] Rembrandt's own version of the scene (see cat. 3) follows both

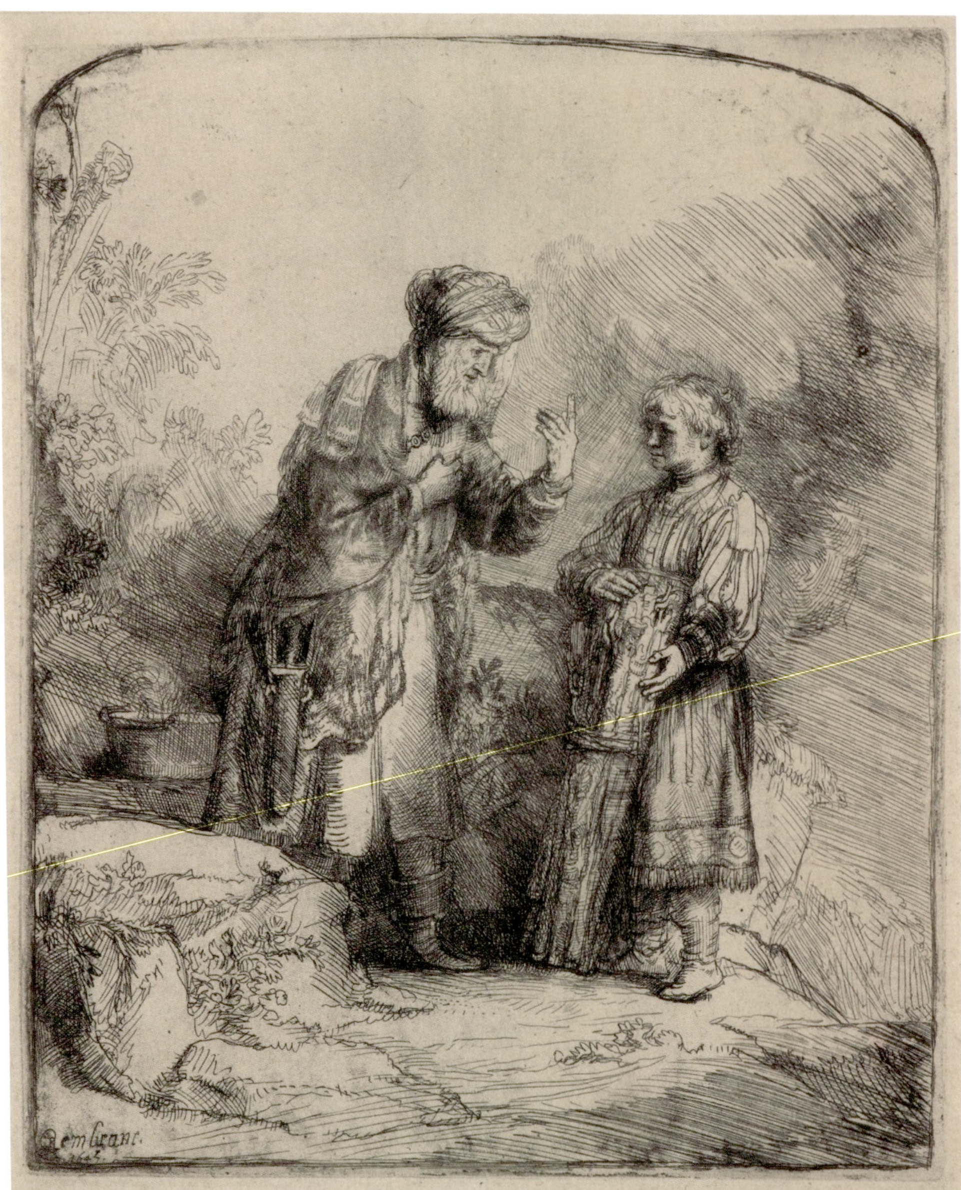

Cat. 4

Rembrandt, *Abraham and Isaac*, 1645
Etching and burin, state i/ii
6 ⅛ × 5 ⅛ inches (15.7 × 13 cm)
The Morgan Library & Museum, New York (RvR 42)

Lucas and Lastman in portraying Hagar and Ishmael as victims. In addition, he includes a cackling Sarah and a smug young Isaac, identifying them as both the beneficiaries and perpetrators of this misfortune.[10] While Hagar weeps, Ishmael's expression is obscured. He is turned away from the viewer, and his body language suggests a stoic demeanor, as if he is resolutely marching off into the wilderness with foresight of his destiny as father of a great nation. While this scene is characterized by both physical motion and intense emotion, suspension lies at its heart: Abraham's conflicted feelings bring him to a standstill on the threshold of his home, his outstretched arms signifying helpless inaction.[11]

In an etching of 1645 depicting another episode from the Abraham narrative—the moment that immediately precedes Abraham's near-sacrifice of Isaac—Rembrandt presents a scene characterized emphatically by both stasis and anticipation (cat. 4). For this work, the artist draws from Genesis 22, as well as from an additional source: a history of the Jews written in the first century by the Jewish scholar Flavius Josephus.[12] In the text of the Bible, Isaac, not knowing the real reason for his and Abraham's journey to a mountain in Moriah, remarks, "Behold the fire and the wood, but where is the lamb for the burnt offering?" His father answers simply that the Lord will provide the lamb. In his account, Josephus expands upon this exchange, writing that, after reaching the mountaintop, Abraham confesses to his son the true nature of the sacrifice they will make, and Isaac willingly accepts his fate. In

Rembrandt's etching, Isaac stands at the edge of the precipice, listening carefully to his father and holding the wood they will use to make the fire. Scholars have pointed to this work as a chief example of Rembrandt's move away from dramatic action in the 1640s.[13] Its subject is the verbal, not the visual—an exchange between a speaker and a listener.[14] Physical movement is limited to a single gesture, Abraham's finger pointing to the unseen Lord above, while Isaac, motionless and expressionless, seems almost not to react. His understanding instead manifests in the shifting light, which casts a shadow on his impassive face, while clouds gather around father and son in anticipation of the sacrifice and salvation imminently to follow.

In the third Abraham etching Rembrandt made between 1637 and 1645, usually called *Abraham Caressing Isaac* (cat. 5),[15] Rembrandt portrays the elderly Abraham holding his young son in his arms, his outward stare—a common anticipatory device in the artist's work—alluding to the sacrifice eventually demanded of him. An obliviously happy Isaac holds an apple, a probable allusion to Christ's sacrifice and redemption of Original Sin, the sacrifice of Isaac being its most commonly invoked typological prefiguration.[16] Another possibility is that this figural group represents Abraham with Ishmael, the first son he will be commanded to "sacrifice," the apple doubling as a quotation of that held by Ishmael in Lucas van Leyden's depiction of the banishment scene (see fig. 2). The ambiguity may also be intentional, referring to both boys at once.

Cat. 5

Rembrandt, *Abraham Caressing Isaac*, ca. 1637–45
Etching, state i/iv
4 ½ × 3 ½ inches (11.6 × 8.9 cm)
The Morgan Library & Museum, New York (RvR 40)

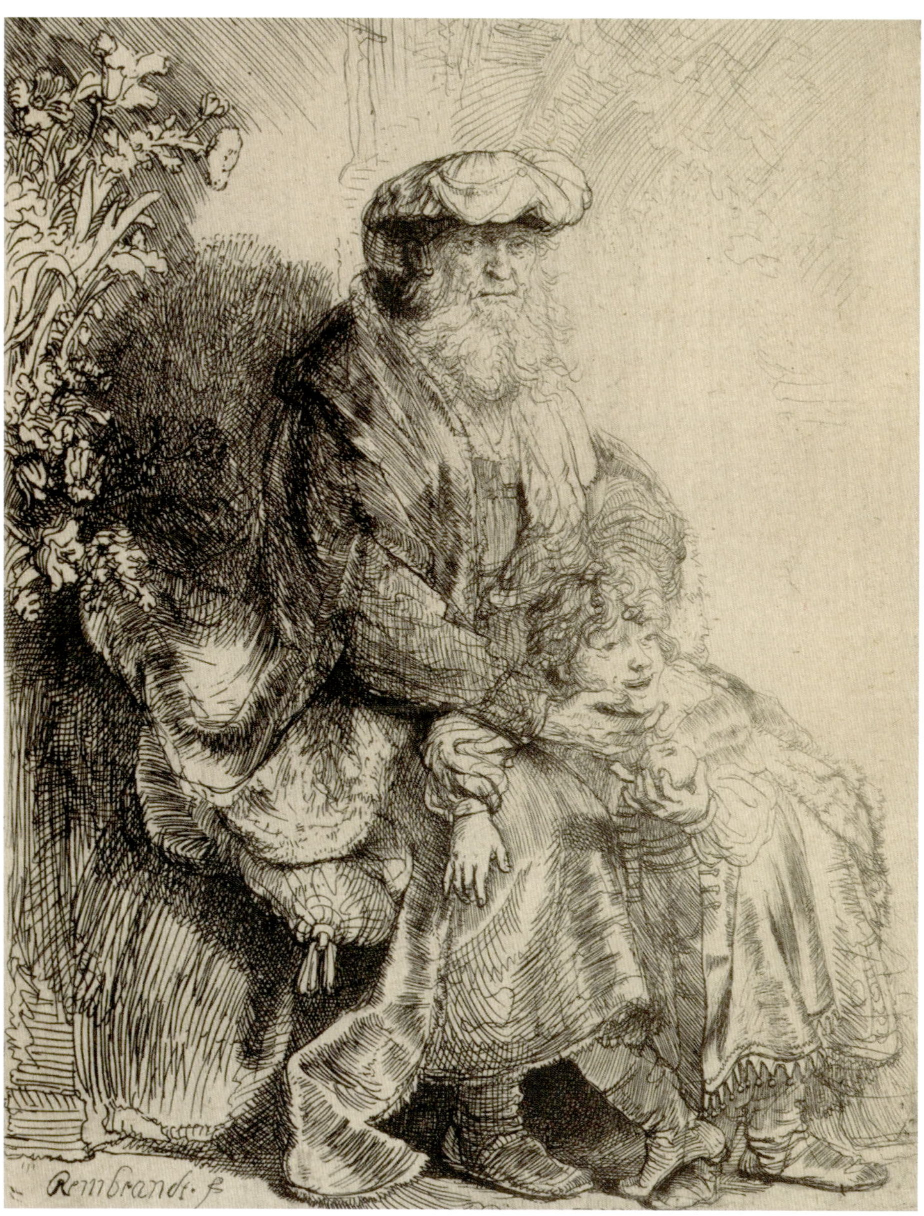

Notably, the 1679 inventory of Clement de Jonghe's collection of Rembrandt's copper plates lists this one as "Father Abraham playing with his son," with no reference to either Isaac or Ishmael.[17] In any case, this image depicts no specific biblical episode and no action whatsoever. It is instead a distillation of the patriarch's affection for a beloved son that alludes to, rather than pictures, the specific events recounted in the Bible. The hands that bear the knife and press down on Isaac's face in the *Sacrifice* and reach out impotently in *Abraham Casting Out Hagar and Ishmael* here caress the boy's cheek and stroke his hair. Making direct eye contact with the viewer, Abraham steps out of the temporal reality of the image and into our own, pointing to the dramatic irony of the boy's sense of security in his father's arms. It is the stillness of the image—the suspension of action—that permits this projection into the future.

In all three of these prints, Rembrandt focuses on the dynamics of foresight rather than physical vision, moving away from dramatic action and reaction in favor of the quietly anticipatory—the defining quality of his next treatment of the Abraham story.

THE UNFOLDING OF A REVELATION

In Rembrandt's *Abraham Entertaining the Angels* of 1646 (see cat. 1), the instantaneity and dynamism of the monumental *Sacrifice of Isaac* of eleven years earlier vanish completely. Now all is calm and hushed. There are no extreme facial expressions, no sudden movements of the body, nothing falls or spills—Abraham is in full control of the pitcher and dish in his hands. Sarah, in the doorway behind him, stands motionless. Even the sky and air are still. The momentousness of the event depicted—a foretelling of the birth of the child through whom God will extend his covenant—is contained within a panel fewer than nine inches wide and conveyed solely by light and a single raised hand.

Responding to the ambiguities of the visitation scene related in Genesis 18, early commentaries on the text sought to explain the identities of Abraham's visitors. Talmudic and other early Jewish writings maintained that Abraham was visited both by the Lord and by three travelers who were in truth the archangels Gabriel, Raphael, and Michael, the last of whom was charged with making the announcement of Isaac's birth.[18] In contrast, early Christian writers, committed to the concept of a Trinitarian God, viewed this and other appearances of the Lord (theophanies) in the Old Testament as evidence of the existence of the Son of God before the Incarnation.[19] They proposed that it was a pre-incarnate Christ, serving as mediator and messenger of God the Father and accompanied by two angels, who appeared to Abraham.[20] At the beginning of the fifth century, however, the highly influential theologian Augustine of Hippo rejected such readings of the Old Testament theophanies, disputing in particular the idea that the Son served in a subordinate role to the Father.[21] For Augustine, Genesis 18, with its vacillation between three travelers and one Lord, between the use of "they" and "he," was itself evidence of the Trinity—Father, Son, and Holy Spirit united in the One God. He writes that while Abraham saw three men, he immediately understood that he was in the presence of the Lord. Augustine thus makes a distinction between physical sight and inner vision.[22] The theologian offered a way of understanding Abraham's visual experience but nevertheless left it to artists, faced with the task of putting this encounter in pictorial form, to decide whether to show what Abraham saw with his eyes or what he knew in his heart.

Depictions of the episode—from the earliest extant example, dating from the fourth century, to such early seventeenth-century works as Lastman's version of 1616 (fig. 3)—almost invariably show three undifferentiated figures, sometimes with wings or haloes, at other times with no indication of their divine status.[23] A remarkable exception appears in one of the fifth-century mosaics in the basilica of Santa Maria Maggiore in Rome (fig. 4).[24] This mosaic contains three vignettes, each representing a different moment of Genesis 18: the visitors' arrival and initial appearance to Abraham; Abraham's instruction to Sarah to prepare the meal; and Abraham serving his guests, presumably while hearing the divine announcement of Isaac's birth. All three visitors possess haloes, but in the first

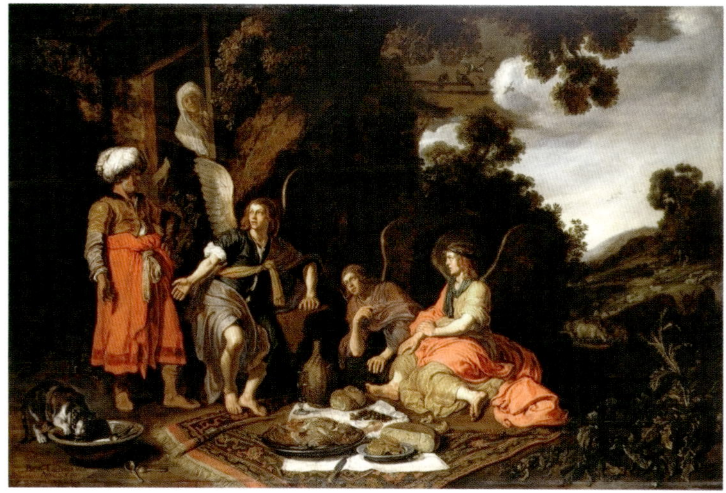

Fig. 3 Pieter Lastman (1583–1633), *Abraham Entertaining the Angels*, 1616. Oil on panel, 32 ¾ × 49 ⅝ inches (82 × 126 cm). Museumslandschaft Hessen Kassel, Gemäldegalerie Alte Meister; on permanent loan from a private collection

vignette one of them is distinguished from the others by an aura of light that encompasses his entire body. This motif—an anticipation of the luminous creature that sits at the center of Rembrandt's painting—does not seem to appear in any of the depictions that followed, which, beginning in the twelfth century, increasingly represented the guests as three winged angels.[25]

The Reformation had no immediate impact on this pictorial tradition, even after the publication, in 1554, of John Calvin's *Commentaries on Genesis*. In this text, the reformer follows the early Christian theologians who believed that Christ himself was among the three visitors, explaining further that he, "the living image of the Father, often appeared to the fathers [meaning the patriarchs of the Old Testament] under the form of an angel, while, at the same time, he yet had angels, of whom he was the Head, for his attendants."[26] Calvin also argues that Abraham would have made his offer of sustenance and rest to the three strangers only if they

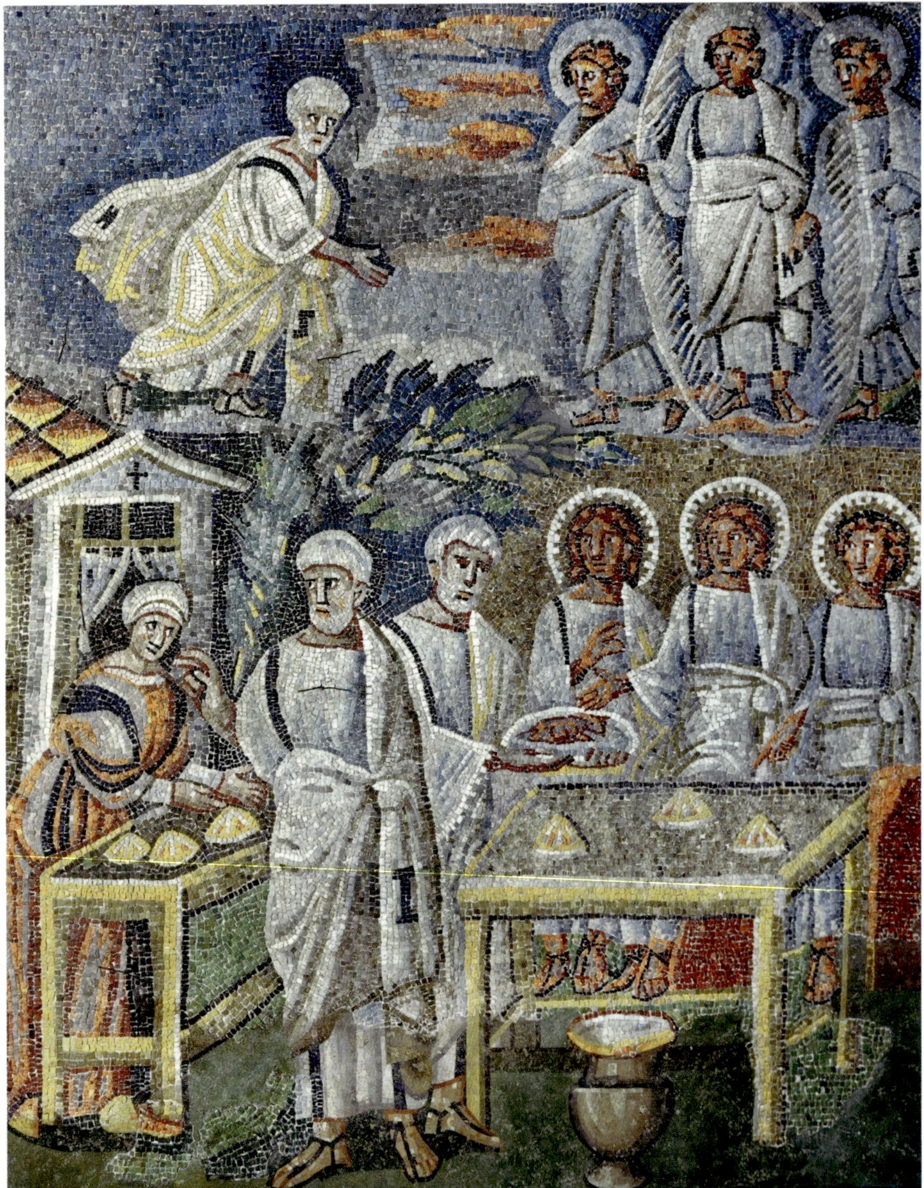

Fig. 4 *Abraham and the Angels*, fifth century. Wall mosaic, Santa Maria Maggiore, Rome

had appeared to him in the form of mortal men, thus differing from Augustine on the point of Abraham's understanding of who the travelers were. An explanatory note in the Dutch States Bible, while making no explicit mention of the Son of God, follows Calvin in identifying the three guests as two angels and the Lord himself, all of whom "took human form for the duration of their visit."[27]

In spite of this, it was not until later in the seventeenth century that Dutch artists regularly depicted the scene with three travelers whose divinity is in no way apparent, opting instead to continue the tradition of three winged angels.[28] Of course, there remained the question of whether one should portray the visitors as they appeared to Abraham or as they really were. One who chose the latter, in unique fashion, was a little-known artist named Jan Barentsz. Muyckens (1595–1665?), whose 1637 print presents the moment the three travelers arrive and first appear to Abraham (fig. 5). This work portrays a Christ-like figure accompanied by two winged angels and is thus a highly unusual instance of an artist putting into visual form the concept of the Son as the living image of the Father in the context of an Old Testament scene. Made the year the Dutch States Bible was first published, this print may be, apart from the Santa Maria Maggiore mosaic, the only work pre-dating Rembrandt's painting that differentiates one of the three travelers.[29]

In his painting, Rembrandt distinguishes one of his three figures not with the facial features conventionally associated with Christ, but

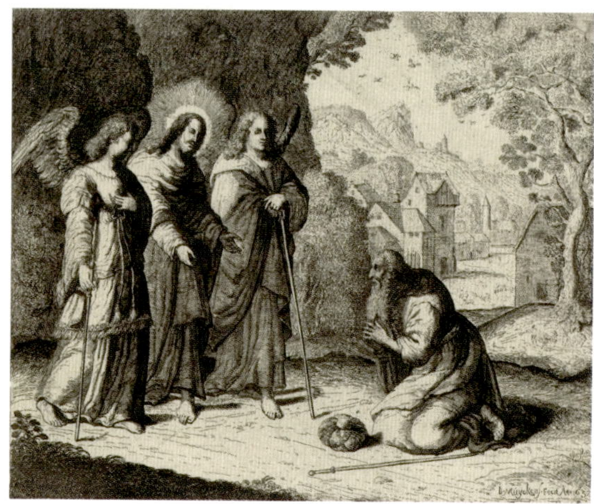

Fig. 5 Jan Barentsz. Muyckens (1595–1665?), *Abraham Greeting the Lord and Two Angels*, 1637. Etching, 7 ½ × 9 ⅛ inches (19.1 × 23.2 cm). Rijksprentenkabinet, Rijksmuseum, Amsterdam

with light (fig. 6). This traditional symbol of the divine had served other artists working around Calvinist restrictions against the representation of God. In Lastman's painting of the Lord's first appearance to Abraham in Genesis 12, for example, beams of light breaking through the trees suffice to indicate the presence of the Lord (fig. 7).[30] In Rembrandt's picture, however, the light does not extend from some unseen source; nor does it radiate around a figure, like the aureole in the Santa Maria Maggiore mosaic (see fig. 4), or like the light accompanying the figure of Christ in Rembrandt's own depictions of the Supper at Emmaus, a New Testament subject with a parallel theme. Instead, the body itself is flush with light; it pulses through the figure's voluminous gown, pooling in its folds and seeping into the cloth on the table.

Rembrandt also uses the light to translate Abraham's revelation into a visual experience, perhaps, in contrast to Calvin, understanding the utterance of the words "Is anything too great for the Lord" to have been accompanied by an actual change in the visitors' appearance, or at least in the patriarch's perception of them. In either case, he shows

Fig. 6 Detail of *Abraham Entertaining the Angels* (cat. 1)

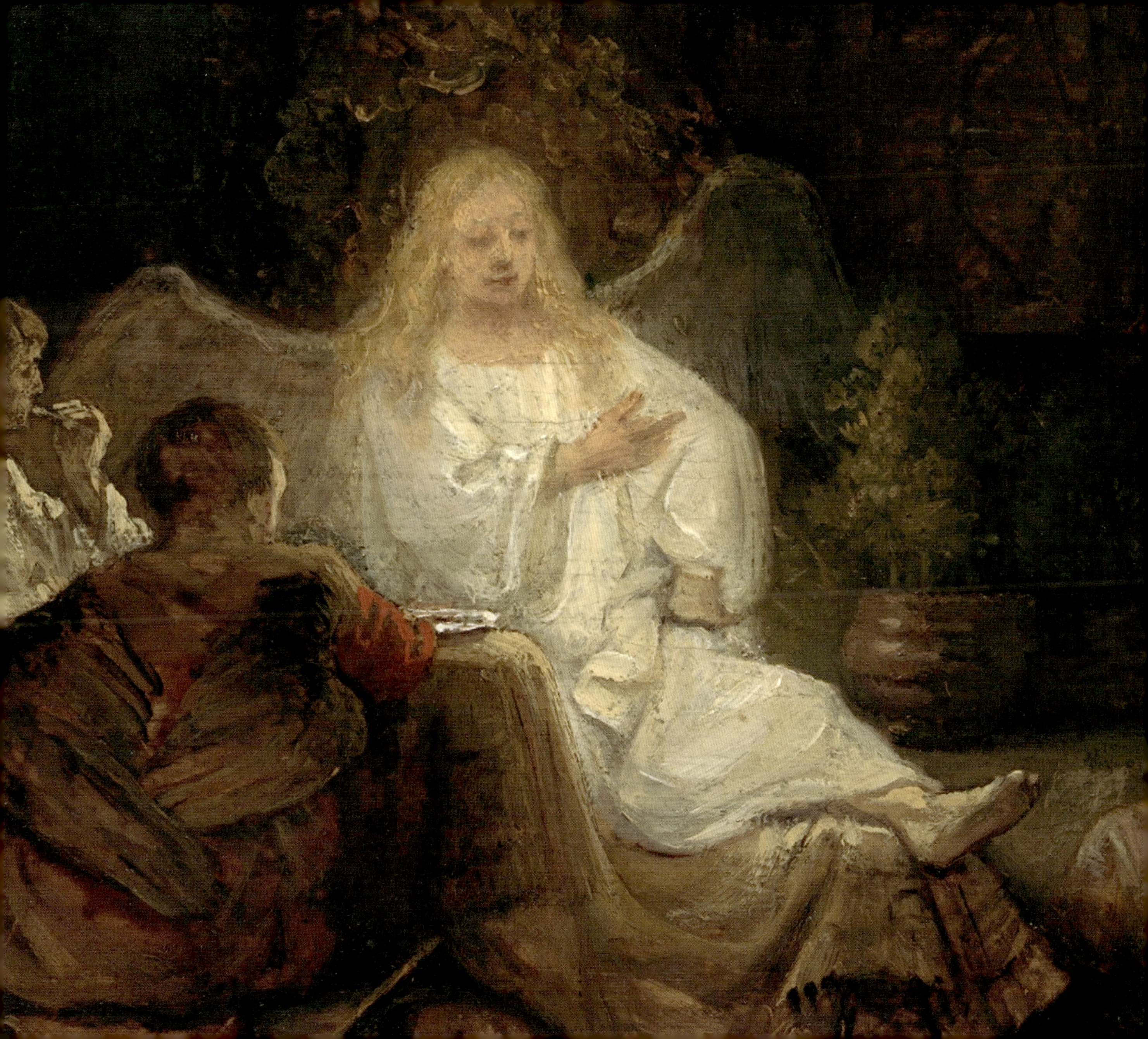

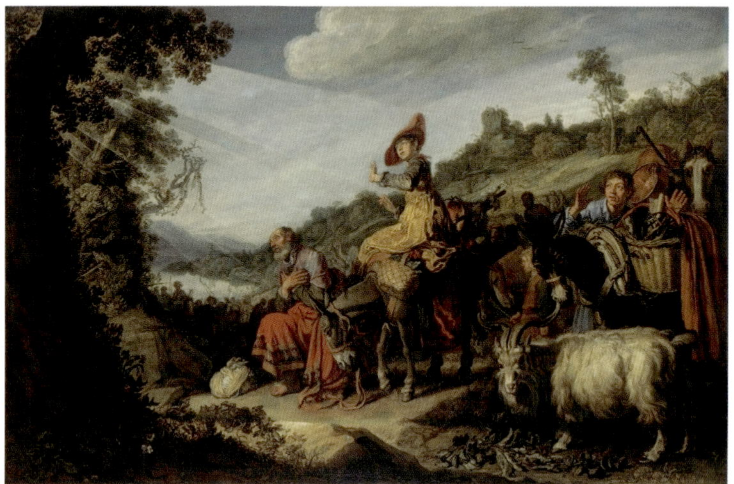

Fig. 7 Pieter Lastman (1583–1633), *Abraham on the Road to Canaan*, 1614. Oil on canvas, 28 5/16 × 48 inches (72 × 122 cm). State Hermitage Museum, St. Petersburg

human flesh transforming into the divine before Abraham's eyes. The figure with his back to the viewer, closest to the picture plane, largely retains the appearance of a traveler, his walking stick laid beside him, a dirty foot extending from beneath his robe. His wings are tucked behind his back—visible to us but not to Abraham or Sarah—and the light just barely kisses his forehead, cheek, and right shoulder (fig. 8). The figure at left who is eating—a sign, according to Calvin, of the flesh-and-blood form the divine could inhabit—raises his wings and receives more of the light, his hand and chest glowing brightly. Finally, the radiant figure at center spreads his wings, showing in vivid visual form the full unfolding of the revelation. His otherworldly luminescence, the primary light source for the entire scene, casts glinting reflections on the dish and pitcher that Abraham holds and sheds a soft glow on the patriarch's arm, while not reaching Sarah at all (fig. 9).

As in Rembrandt's earlier Abraham etchings, reaction manifests not as action but as the cessation thereof. The patriarch, who has kneeled

Fig. 8 Detail of *Abraham Entertaining the Angels* (cat. 1)

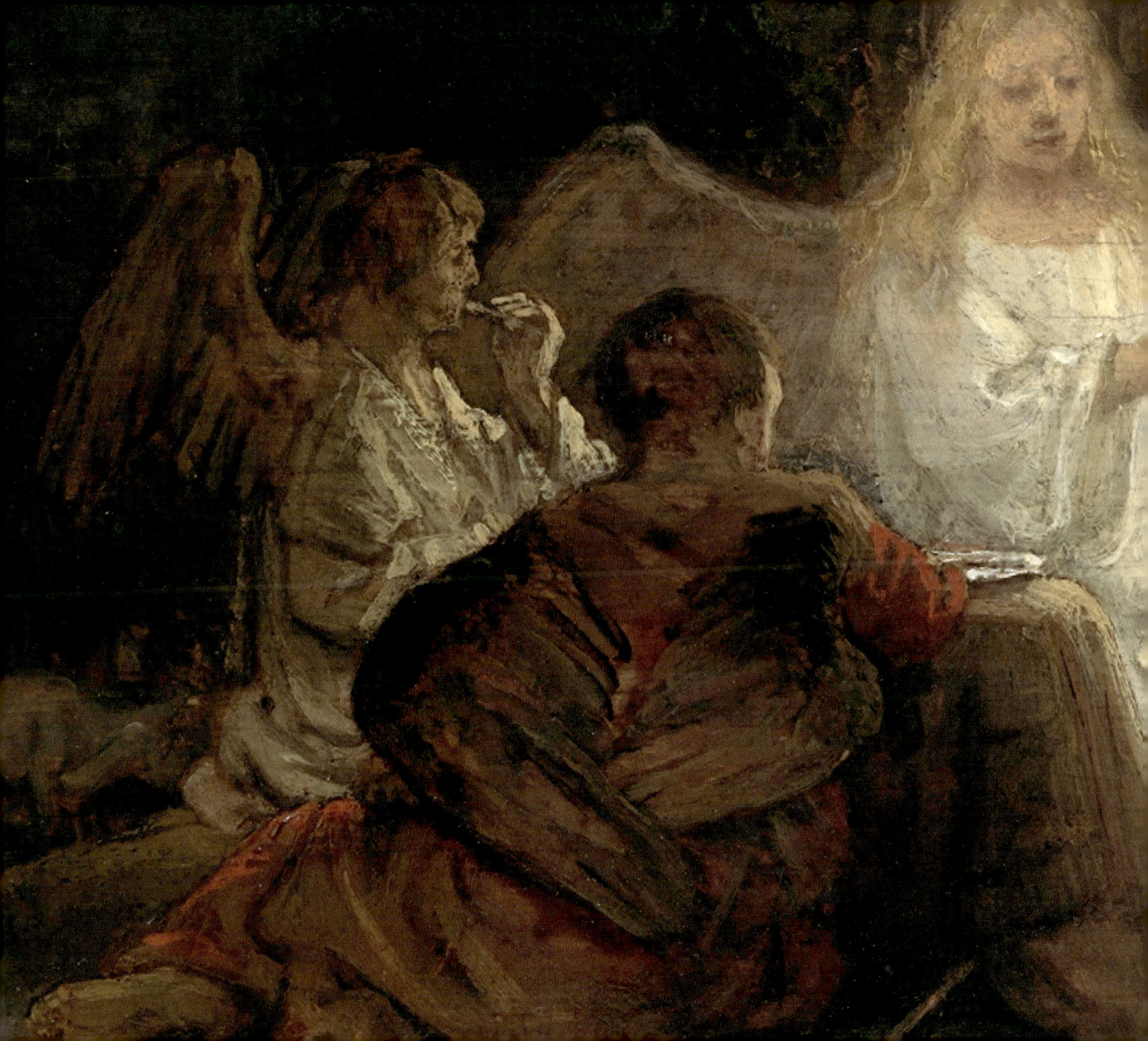

to wash his guests' feet (as in the biblical text), stops, his thumb poised on the lid of the pitcher, and simply listens. His face is receptive but impassive. Sarah, whose laughter and disbelief are in large part the focus of the biblical passage, also shows no discernible expression. Neither has yet fully grasped what has been revealed. In this way, in complete contrast to his *Sacrifice of Isaac* from 1635, Rembrandt extends the dramatic moment, showing a lapse between action and reaction, between the reversal of fortune and the recognition.[31]

Put another way, the stasis, or suspension, in this image conveys a disconnect between sensory perception and cognition, between sensing and understanding—completely contrary to Augustine's notion of Abraham's immediate inner vision. In Rembrandt's reading of the story, Abraham and Sarah are both deceived by what they see. They take the three travelers at face value, and the result is doubt—disbelief in the prophetic announcement of Isaac's birth.

The potential of the visual, of sight itself, to deceive was a concept prevalent in the scientific, religious, artistic, and philosophical discourses of the period. Advances in science had led to a new understanding of optics and the mechanism of the eye, as well as of the distortions of human vision.[32] At the same time, against the backdrop of an unprecedented proliferation of visual imagery, only decades after infamous outbreaks of iconoclasm in the name of Calvinism, the illusory and seductive power of painting became a preoccupation among

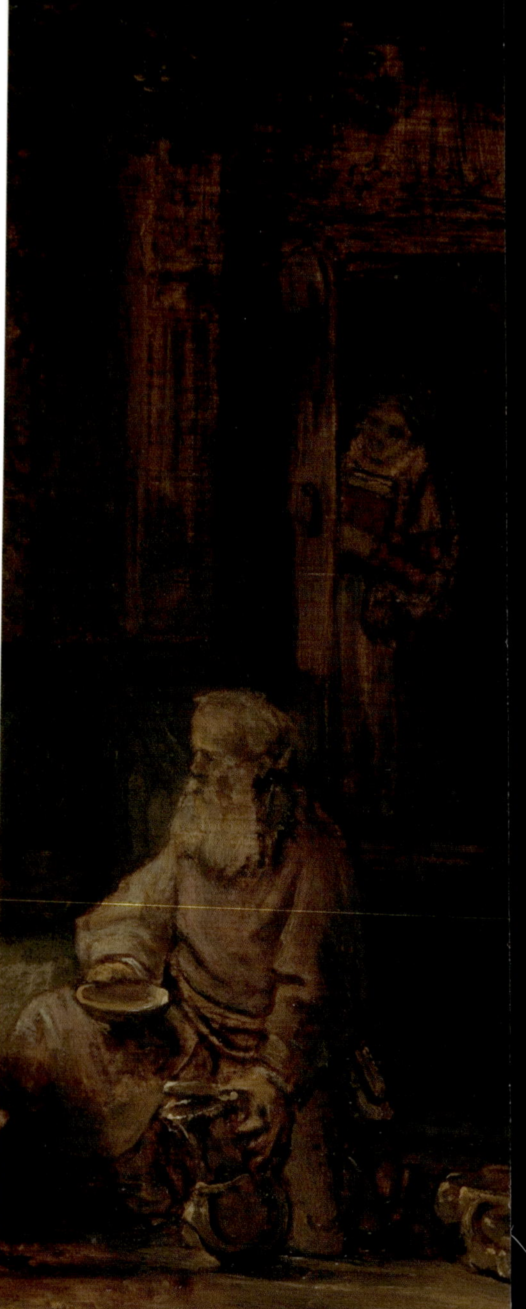

art lovers and moralists, one side celebrating it, the other pointing to its dangers.[33] In addition, in his writings of the 1630s and 1640s, the French-born philosopher, and resident of the Dutch Republic, René Descartes (1596—1650) formulated his highly influential mind-body dualism, specifically with regard to proving the existence of God.[34] While addressing all the senses, he focused largely on sight, articulating a new, complex causal relationship between the eye and the mind. For Descartes, doubt in God was the product of the failure to distinguish between the physical and the immaterial, and of the resulting reliance on the senses for knowledge:

> But what convinces many people that there is a problem in knowing Him [God], and even of knowing what their soul is, is that they never raise their mind above the realm of sensory things and are so used not to think of anything except by imagining it, which is a mode of thinking peculiar to material objects, that everything which seems unimaginable seems to them unintelligible. This is clear enough from the fact that even scholastic philosophers hold as a maxim that there is nothing in the intellect which has not previously been in the senses, in which, however, it is certain that the ideas of God and the soul have never been.[35]

Whether or not Rembrandt consciously incorporated Cartesian ideas into his religious imagery, with *Abraham Entertaining the Angels* of 1646,

Fig. 9 Detail of *Abraham Entertaining the Angels* (cat. 1)

he undertook his own investigation of the relationship between sensing and knowing, one that yielded a new understanding of "the most natural motions" of body and mind.

THE IMMATERIALITY OF THE DIVINE

In the 1650s, Rembrandt produced a number of other works treating episodes from the Abraham narrative. Among them are two images, a drawing and an etching, in which he reprises the subject of Isaac's sacrifice. In the drawing, he completely discards the graceful poses and fluttering drapery of his 1635 painting of the subject and instead emphasizes the brutality of this scene of filicide (cat. 6). A frail Abraham, seen from the back, leans over Isaac's body with bent legs. He covers his son's mouth, stopping his cries, but does not block his eyes from the sight of the knife being brought to his throat. So steadfast is Abraham in his fulfillment of God's command—so blind is his faith—that he remains unaware of the angel hovering above him, senseless to the hand placed on his head and deaf to the words that issue from the angel's open mouth.[36]

In the etching (cat. 7), Rembrandt transports certain elements from the drawing—the angel's parted lips and the dramatic stream of light that accompanies this divine being—but he produces an image with an entirely different dynamic and feeling. In accordance with Josephus's

Cat. 6

Rembrandt, *Sacrifice of Isaac*, ca. 1652–54
Pen and brown ink on paper
7 ⅛ × 6 ⅛ inches (18 × 15.5 cm)
Kupferstichkabinett, Staatliche
Kunstsammlungen Dresden

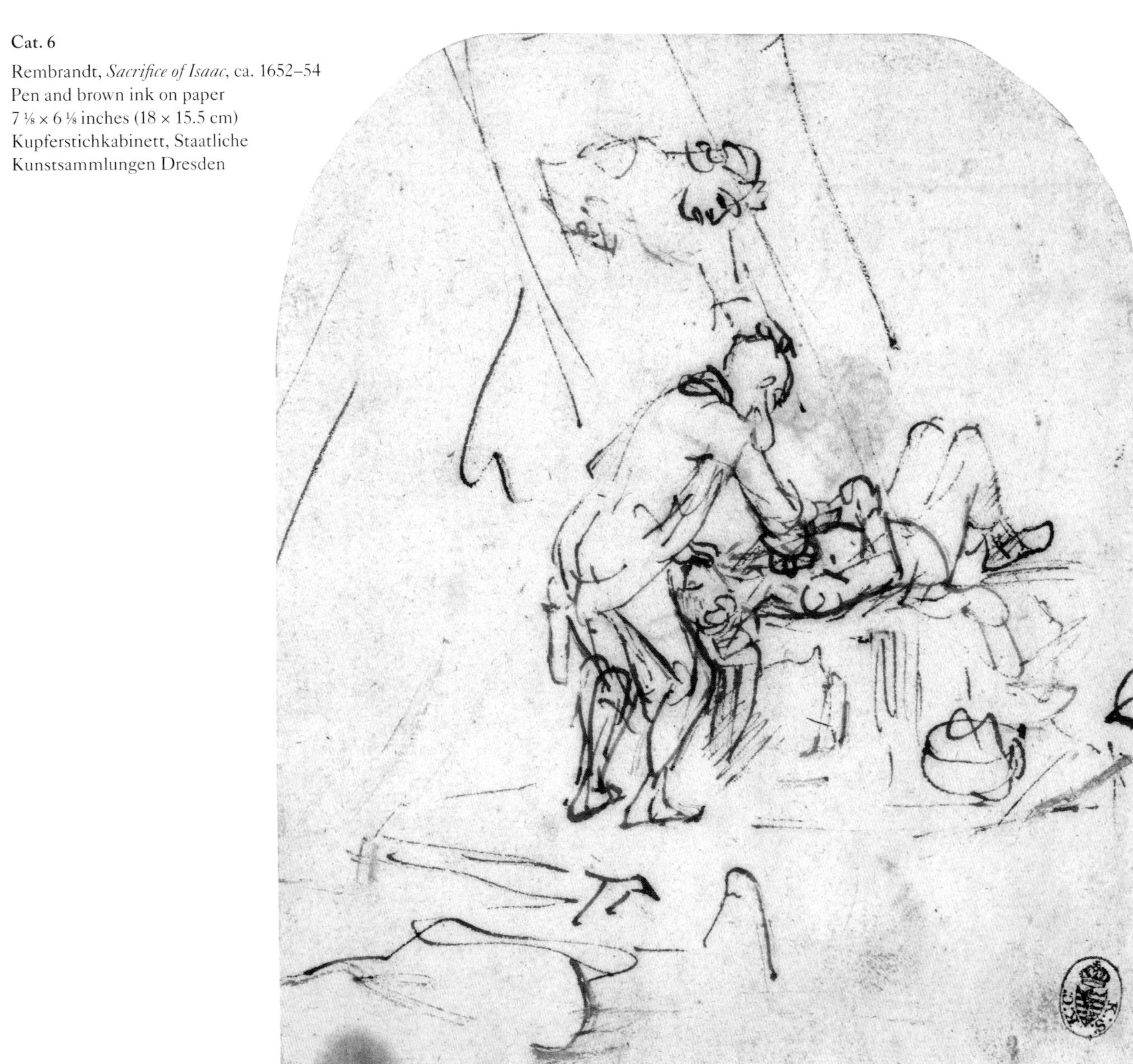

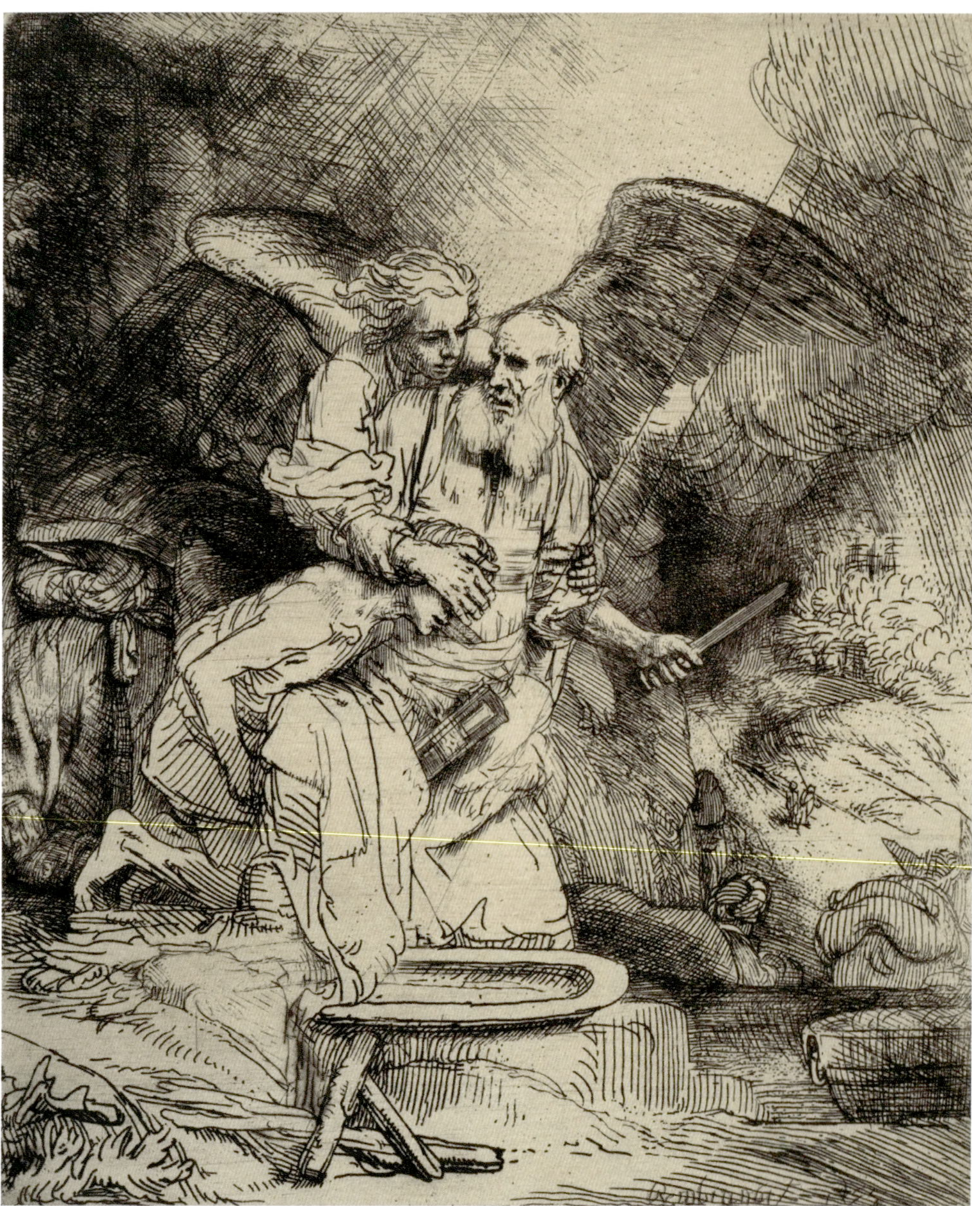

Cat. 7

Rembrandt, *Sacrifice of Isaac*, 1655
Etching and drypoint, only state
6 ⅛ × 5 ⅛ inches (15.6 × 13.1 cm)
The Metropolitan Museum of Art, New York; Bequest of Ida Kammerer, in memory of her husband, Frederic Kammerer (M.D., 1933)

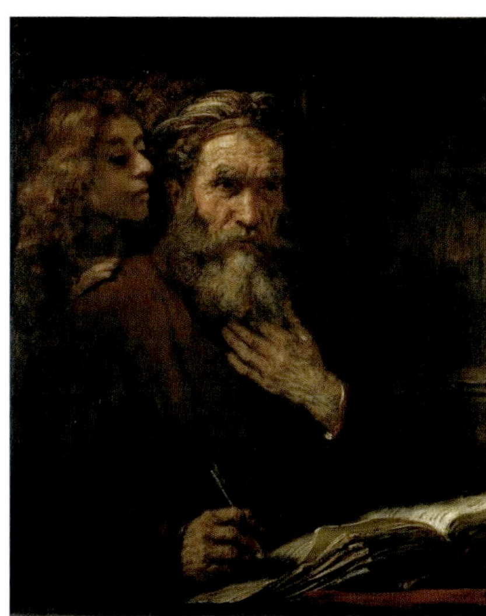

Fig. 10 Rembrandt, *St. Matthew and the Angel*, 1661. Oil on canvas, 38 × 32 inches (96 × 81 cm). Musée du Louvre, Paris

account and Rembrandt's own 1645 etching of Abraham and Isaac before the sacrifice (see cat. 4), the boy is now a willing participant, kneeling cooperatively with his hands unbound.[37] Abraham covers only his son's eyes, a gesture more protective than violent. This tenderness is echoed by the angel's embrace of Abraham, its wings sheltering father, son, and, at left, the ram that God, to the patriarch's surprise, ultimately provides as a replacement for Isaac.

Unlike in the drawing, here Abraham is not completely senseless to the intervention. He reacts, turning his head and pausing in his action, knife in hand, his open mouth suggesting confusion. Within the deep shadows surrounding them, the whites of the patriarch's eyes are discernible upon close inspection, but Abraham nevertheless seems not to see the angel.[38] Instead, he sees through this angelic body to the ram that is almost hidden from our view. According to the biblical text, after the angel called out to Abraham, the patriarch "looked up and there in the thicket saw a ram." The Dutch States Bible contains an annotation that emphasizes the importance of the animal: "The angel came from behind, so that in turning about he [Abraham] did spy the ram, instantly apprehending that he was to offer the same in his son's stead."[39] With his rendering of Abraham's gaze and expression, Rembrandt does not show the instant apprehension described in the text, but he does identify the ram as the visible, flesh-and-blood sign of the invisible, immaterial angel.[40]

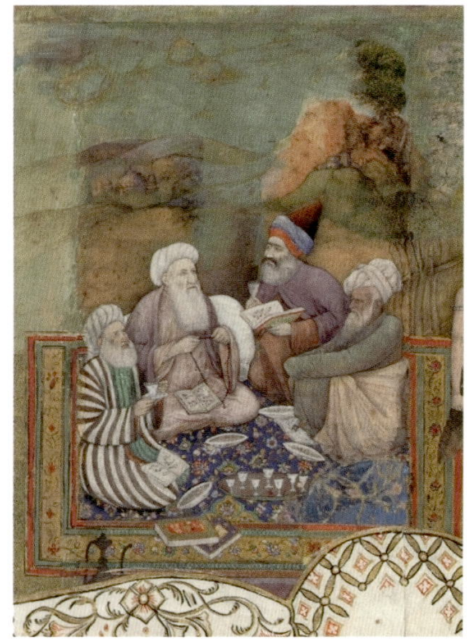

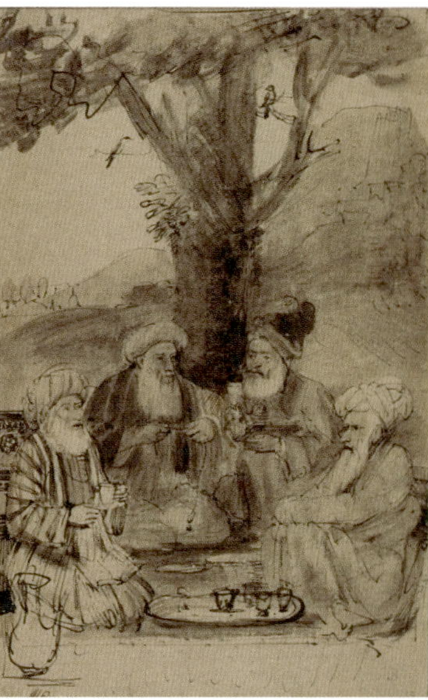

Fig. 11 *Four Sufi Mystics*, Mughal empire, 1627–28. Opaque watercolor on paper, approximately 7 ¼ × 5 ⅝ inches (18.4 × 14.3 cm). Schloss Schönbrunn and the Imperial Apartments of the Vienna Hofburg

Fig. 12 Rembrandt, *Four Men Seated under a Tree*, ca. 1656. Pen and ink with wash on paper, 7 ⅝ × 4 ⅞ inches (19.4 × 12.4 cm). The British Museum, London

The artist would take a very similar approach in his later *St. Matthew and the Angel* (fig. 10), in which a youthful angelic figure approaches the apostle from behind, places a hand on his shoulder, and whispers in his ear.[41] Light washes over Matthew's face and his open book, and he touches his wrinkled hand to his chest in a gesture of understanding. The apostle thus receives the divine inspiration offered to him, on some level hearing and feeling the angel's presence but seeing nothing. In this painting and in his drawing and etching of the *Sacrifice*, Rembrandt situates angels in the realm of the immaterial, while the mortals in these images possess varying degrees of awareness of their presence, from complete ignorance to partial awareness to full understanding. In this exploration of cognizance independent of sight, the artist both draws on and departs from the Calvinist exegesis of the States Bible, perhaps also

Cat. 8

Rembrandt, *Abraham Entertaining the Angels*, 1656
Etched copper plate with drypoint
6 ⅜ × 5 ¼ inches (16.2 × 13.3 cm)
National Gallery of Art, Washington;
Gift of Ladislaus and Beatrix von Hoffmann and Patrons' Permanent Fund

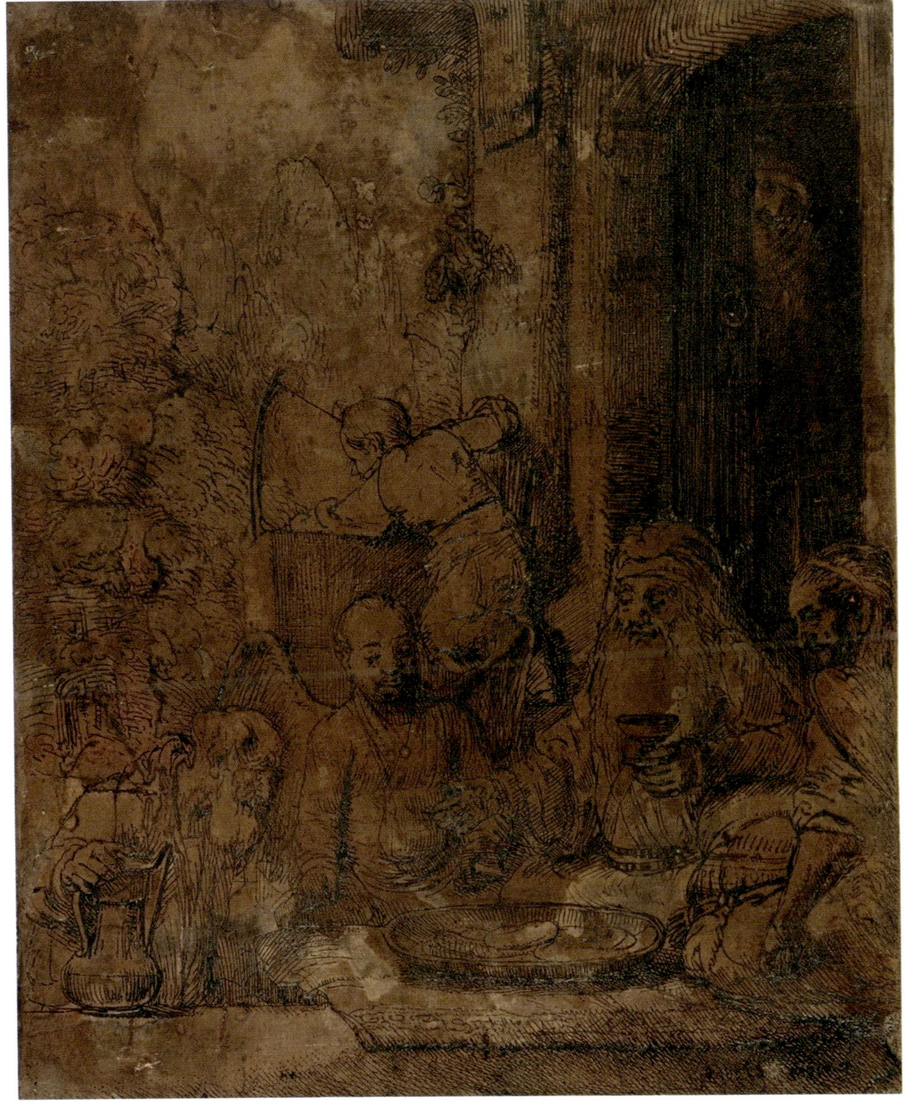

inspired by the Cartesian distinction between the body and the mind, the eye and the intellect.

SIGHT VERSUS FAITH

In the year following the *Sacrifice of Isaac* of 1655, Rembrandt made his etched version of the visitation scene in Genesis 18 (see cat. 2). In contrast to his painting of this scene from 1646, the artist now emphatically identifies one of the figures as the Lord himself, a shift that is indicative of his new understanding of revelation as a non-visual experience.[42]

The artist based the composition of this print on an early seventeenth-century Mughal painting of four Sufi mystics (fig. 11) that was, in the eighteenth century, cut and incorporated into a larger composition as part of the wall decoration of the Millionenzimmer in the Schloss Schönbrunn, Vienna.[43] Rembrandt copied, and most likely owned, this work and a number of other Mughal paintings (typically called miniatures).[44] His drawing after this particular example (fig. 12) may postdate the 1656 print, which more closely follows the asymmetric arrangement of the figures.[45] The etching is the only instance in which he employed a Mughal miniature as a model for a finished work. Although far from certain, a relationship between the content of the miniature and that of Rembrandt's print is possible. A number of individuals in the Dutch Republic, particularly in his hometown of

Leiden—a center of Arabic studies—could have helped him to understand the subject of the Mughal image, given the inscriptions that identify the four mystics.[46] Perhaps the artist was even aware of the Islamic ideal, toward which Sufis strive, to worship Allah "as though you see him."

In any case, upon encountering the Mughal work, Rembrandt must have noted its resemblance to his *Abraham Entertaining the Angels* of 1646 (see cat. 1), itself executed on a nearly miniature scale. Like his painting, the Mughal image features four figures seated around a meal service, with a prominently placed pitcher, and, although it is no longer visible because of the eighteenth-century intervention, a tree at center. The miniature is also similarly characterized by stasis.[47] Comparison with the copper plate on which Rembrandt composed his etching (cat. 8)—a rare example of a plate that was spared from continual reprinting and reworking in later centuries and therefore preserves the artist's original etched lines[48]—shows his transposition of the Mughal composition into his religious scene. He turns the leftmost figure (the rightmost in the final print) into Abraham, the adjacent man and the one farthest to the right into two winged angels, and the fourth into the figure of the Lord. To this group, he adds Sarah in the doorway and, at center, his back to the viewer, Ishmael.

The highly unusual if not unprecedented inclusion of Ishmael is key to an understanding of the image as a whole.[49] Scholars have connected his presence to the apostle Paul's identification of Ishmael as an allegory of the Jews who did not accept Christ as the Messiah and who, in the

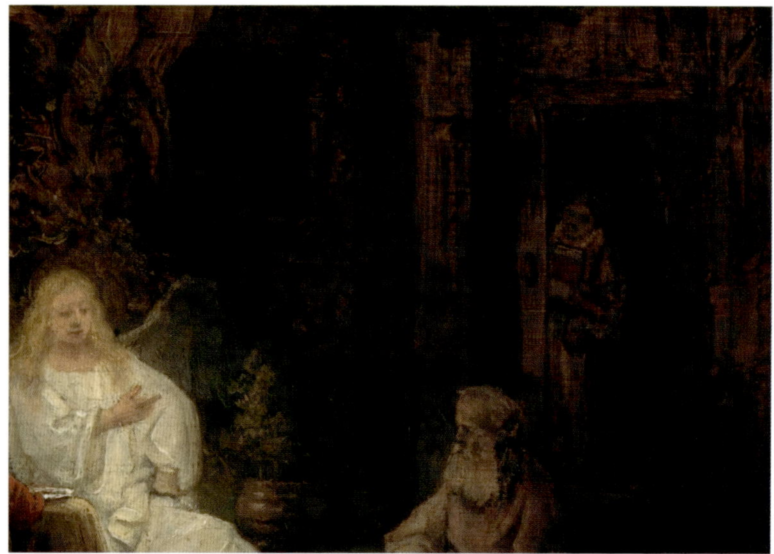

Fig. 13 Detail of *Abraham Entertaining the Angels* (cat. 1)

apostle's view, turned their backs to God.[50] As we have seen, however, in his *Abraham Casting Out Hagar and Ishmael* (see cat. 3), Rembrandt, like others before him, disregarded this reading in favor of one that is more sympathetic toward Abraham's firstborn. As Michael Zell has discussed, Rembrandt's print of 1656 may instead relate to a revision of the Pauline interpretation by the seventeenth-century theologian Paul Felgenhauer, which called for rapprochement between Jews and Christians, both of whom could, in his words, "possess the spirit, faith and Obedience of Abraham . . . One in One."[51] Felgenhauer belonged to an interfaith group of contemporary millenarians—Christian and Jewish thinkers who believed in the imminent coming of the Messiah—and his text was published in 1655 by the prominent Amsterdam rabbi and Jewish apologist Menasseh ben Israel.[52] In the same year, Menasseh produced his own messianic text, *Piedra gloriosa*, for which Rembrandt produced

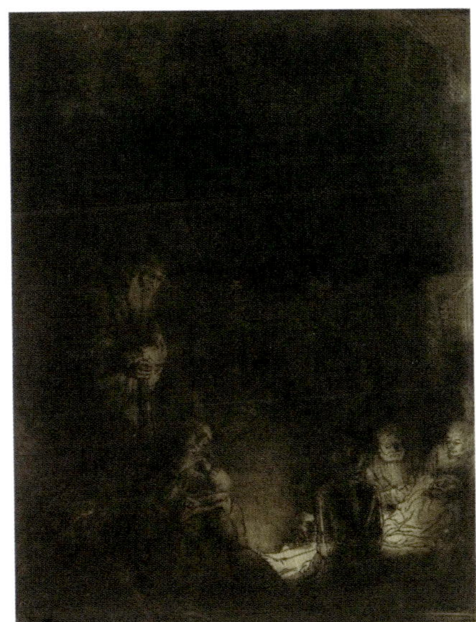

Fig. 14 Rembrandt, *The Entombment*, ca. 1654.
Etching and drypoint and plate tone on vellum, state ii/iv,
8 1/16 × 6 1/4 inches (20.5 × 15.8 cm).
Rijksprentenkabinet, Rijksmuseum, Amsterdam

four illustrations.[53] While Menasseh would not have shared the notion of Ishmael as an allegory of the Jewish people, he references Genesis 18 and describes the Lord promising Abraham that "all the families of the earth shall be blessed in thee, and in thy seed."[54] Whatever his own views on millenarianism, Rembrandt could not have failed to take an interest in the implications of this contemporary discourse for the understanding of Abraham and his two sons.

Furthermore, in Rembrandt's etching, Ishmael's presence is a harbinger of one of the consequences of Isaac's birth. The artist was probably already thinking about the story in these terms when he made his 1646 painting, in which he includes a bow, Ishmael's attribute, hanging on the side of the house, directly between the angelic God and Abraham (fig. 13).[55] In the etched version, as in the expulsion scene from 1637, Ishmael's placement with his back to the viewer indicates not his turning away from the faith but rather a turning toward his divinely ordained destiny, most immediately toward the wilderness to which he will shortly be forced to flee.

Rembrandt employs light to underscore this dynamic of foresight and understanding but in a manner completely different from that of his painting of 1646. Now setting the scene in the bright light of day, he features no divinely illuminated figure. In no known impression did Rembrandt make use of plate tone to achieve such an effect, as he did in his *Entombment* etching of the same period (fig. 14). Instead,

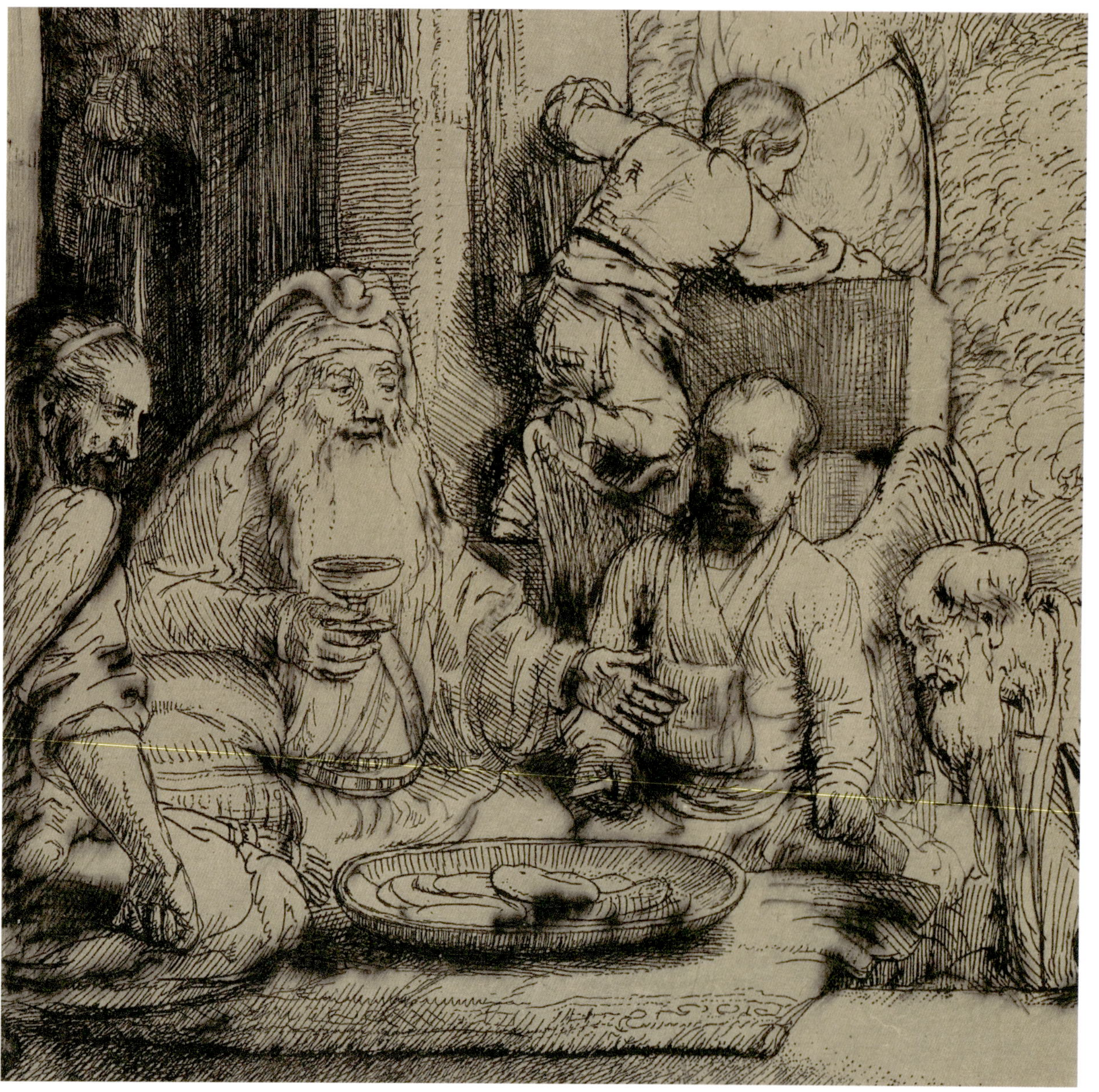

the velvety printed line and burr of a drypoint needle, visible only in early impressions of the print, suggest a subtle play of light and shadow dappling across the figures and objects in the foreground (fig. 15)—a naturalization of divine illumination that, significantly, connects the Lord's open mouth, and his revelatory words, to Abraham and Ishmael but not to Sarah. Instead, Rembrandt expresses the aged woman's doubt by placing her in the shadowy depths of the doorway, rendered with dense crosshatching. Gazing at the guests, she seeks to see and thus fails in her faith. By contrast, Ishmael, brightly lit, looks away, not at all reliant on sight for his belief in the announcement of Isaac's birth or his understanding of its eventual consequences, which he seems already to enact. Between the two extremes is the wizened Abraham, who bows his head and averts his eyes from his guests in order to take in the full significance of this act of divine providence.[56] Rembrandt now directly opposes sight and understanding.

In keeping with this opposition, here the artist portrays the Lord's two companions with an incongruous combination of angelic wings and masculine, bearded faces.[57] This hybridity is not an expression of revelation in progress but a demonstration of their dual identity as the men whom Abraham sees with his eyes and the angels he now knows them to be.[58]

Rembrandt's flesh-and-blood God functions similarly. This figure, who has no wings, accords with longstanding conventions for portraying God

Fig. 15 Detail of *Abraham Entertaining the Angels* (cat. 2)

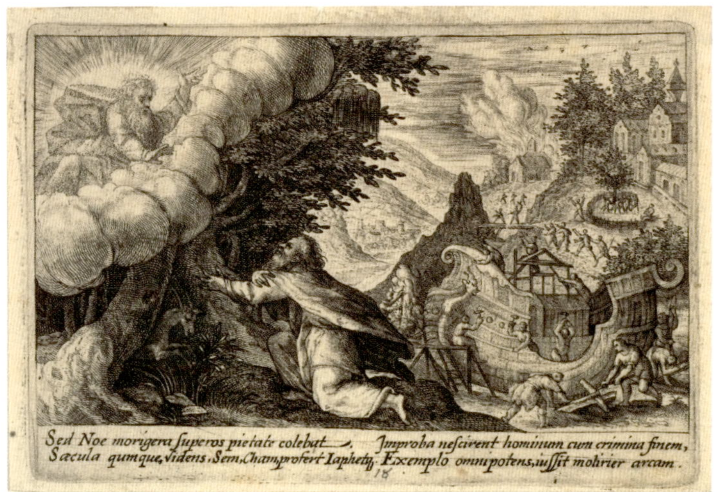

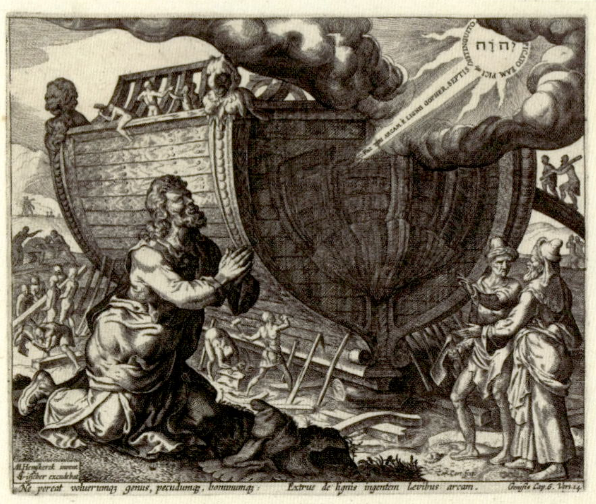

Fig. 16 Crispijn de Passe the Elder (1564–1637), *The Lord Commanding Noah to Build the Ark*, from the *Liber Genesis*, 1612. Engraving, 3 7⁄16 × 5 3⁄16 inches (8.8 × 13.1 cm). The Metropolitan Museum of Art, New York; Bequest of Phyllis Massar, 2011

Fig. 17 Cornelis Cort (1533–1578), after Maarten van Heemskerck (1498–1574), *The Lord Commanding Noah to Build the Ark*, published by Claes Jansz. Visscher (1587–1652), 1643. Engraving, 7 7⁄8 × 9 9⁄16 inches (20 × 24.3 cm). Rijksprentenkabinet, Rijksmuseum, Amsterdam

the Father. In spite of Calvinist restrictions, such corporeal representations of the Lord were not unheard of in seventeenth-century Dutch art: an older bearded deity remained an occasional presence, as, for example, in Crispijn de Passe's 1612 prints for the *Liber Genesis* (fig. 16).[59] More often, however, from the later sixteenth century on, artists in the Northern Netherlands studiously avoided such imagery, replacing likenesses of the Lord with rays of light (as in Lastman's depiction of Genesis 12), an empty aureole, or, frequently, the Tetragrammaton (the Hebrew name for God consisting of four letters) (fig. 17).[60] Rembrandt himself included but ultimately painted over an image of God the Father in his 1636 *Ascension* for Frederik Hendrik, Prince of Orange (Alte Pinakothek, Munich).

In the mid-1650s, however, the artist took a renewed interest in the corporeal representation of God, undoubtedly in connection with contemporary millenarian expectations for the coming of the Messiah—humanity's ultimate encounter with the divine. In addition

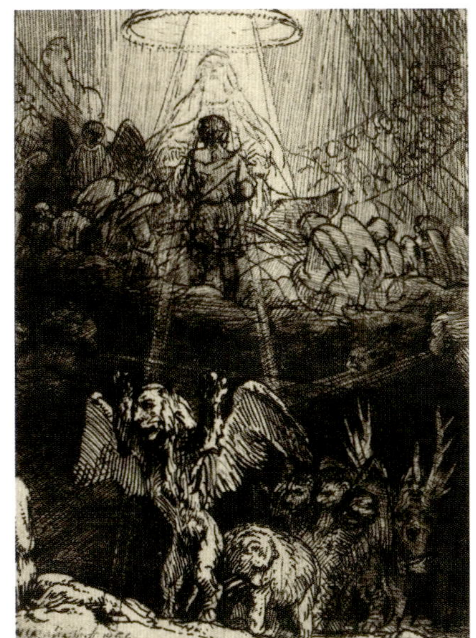

Fig. 18 Rembrandt, *Daniel's Vision of the Four Beasts*, 1655. Etching with drypoint, state ii/iv, 4 3⁄16 × 3 inches (10.7 × 7.6 cm). Rijksprentenkabinet, Rijksmuseum, Amsterdam

to the 1656 print, he had, in the previous year, incorporated a similar representation of the Almighty into *Daniel's Vision of the Four Beasts* (fig. 18), one of the etchings he made for Menasseh ben Israel's *Piedra gloriosa*—a highly unusual instance of a representation of God in a Jewish context.[61] In this work, the depiction of a vision rather than of an actual, earthly encounter, Rembrandt renders the figure, at the top center of the image, with thin etched lines and no modeling, giving him an ethereal, otherworldly appearance.

In contrast, two drawings also made by Rembrandt in the 1650s feature a very physical God in the act of descending to earth. In a large sheet from Dresden (cat. 9), he depicts Genesis 17, another instance in which the Lord "appeared" to Abraham. This momentous episode, in which the covenant is established, anticipates and overlaps with Genesis 18, where Abraham alone hears that he will have a child with Sarah and that this child, Isaac, will inherit God's covenant, while Ishmael will also become the father of a great nation. This passage is less ambiguous than that of 18; it states simply that the Lord appeared and spoke to Abraham, without reference to any dissimulating messengers. There was little visual tradition connected to this episode, but Rembrandt would have been aware of Dirk Coornhert's 1549 engraving after Maarten van Heemskerck (part of a larger print series dedicated to the story of Abraham), in which God appears as a bearded man, aloft and accompanied by angels or cherubim. Rembrandt employs the same iconography in his drawing, in which a

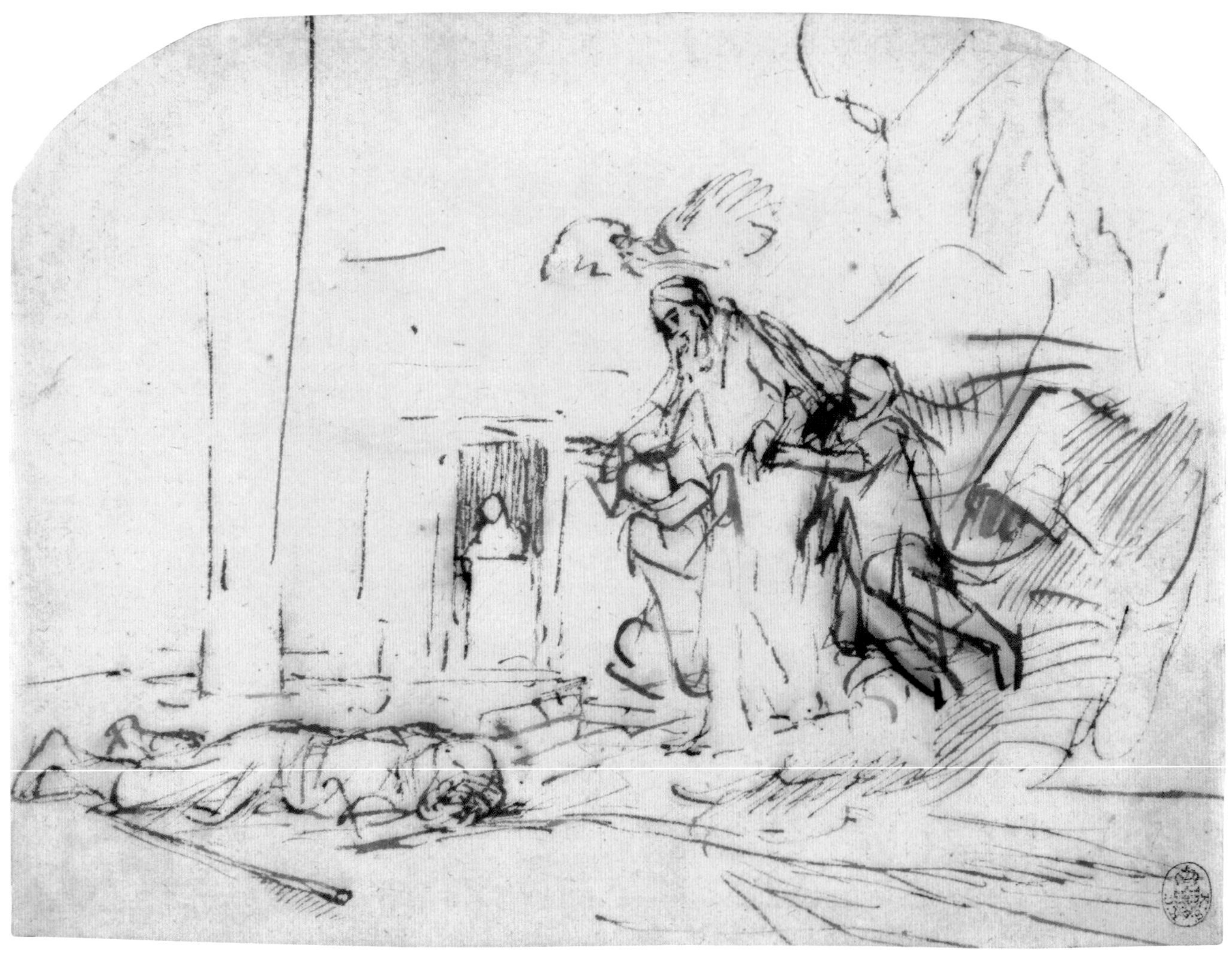

Cat. 9

Rembrandt, *God Making His Covenant with Abraham*, ca. 1656–58
Pen and ink on paper
7 ¾ × 10 ½ inches (19.7 × 26.6 cm)
Kupferstichkabinett, Staatliche Kunstsammlungen Dresden

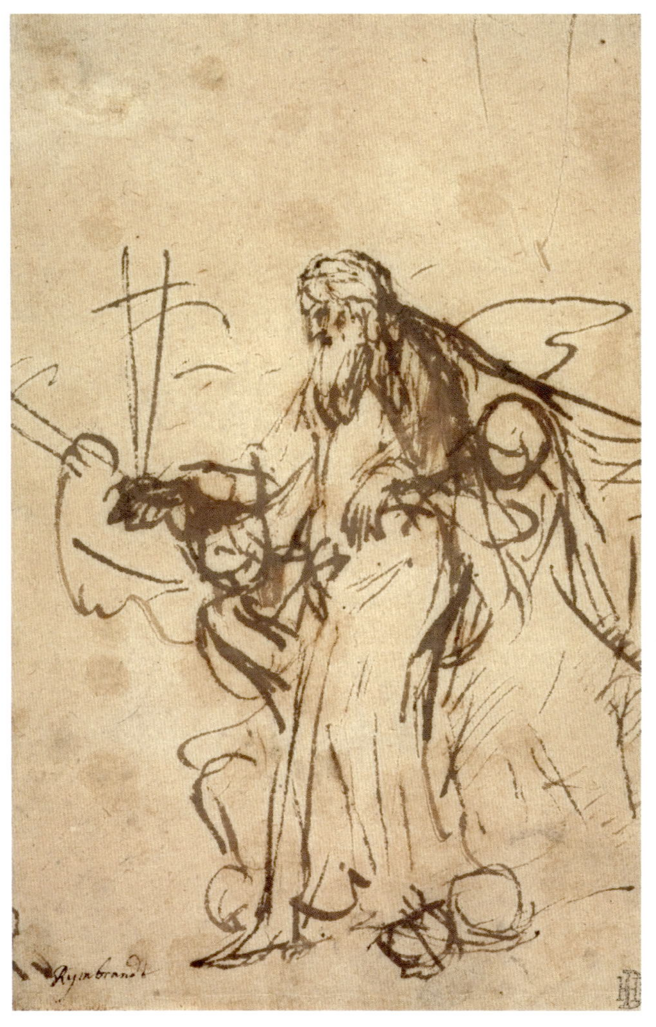

Cat. 10

Rembrandt, *God the Father Supported by Angels*, ca. 1656–58
Pen and brown ink on laid paper
7 15⁄16 × 5 ¼ inches (20.1 × 13.3 cm)
National Gallery of Art, Washington; Widener Collection

divine figure is carried by cherubim and accompanied by swirling clouds and flowing drapery. In a related study dedicated to this figural group, the artist more clearly identifies the central figure as the Lord, elaborating his long beard (cat. 10). He also shows the two winged cherubim bearing the full weight of his body, while his arms hang passively at his sides. In the compositional drawing, Rembrandt follows the biblical text, in which Abraham "falls on his face." Fully prostrate, his face buried in his hands, he does not—cannot—look at the Lord as he takes in this act of divine providence.[62] Rembrandt presents to us what the patriarch knows to be present but cannot see or even envision. Similarly, the figure of God in the *Abraham Entertaining the Angels* etching exists, to use Descartes's terminology, not in the senses or in the imagination but in the intellect. In this image, the only figure who looks in the direction of this visual form, Sarah, fails to perceive the actual presence of the divine.

GENESIS 18 AND REMBRANDT'S CIRCLE

Rembrandt was not alone in his exploration of Genesis 18, the complexities of which lend themselves to diverse treatment. It remained a popular subject throughout the seventeenth century, and his picture from 1646 inspired a number of variations by members of his circle and more distant followers.[63] Among them are works by Ferdinand Bol (1616–1680), who had studied with Rembrandt in the later 1630s and who may have owned his teacher's painting for a period of time; in about 1650, either he or a member of his workshop produced a version of the scene that derives from it (fig. 19).[64] Closely resembling this work is a painting attributed to Jan Victors (1619–1676), a follower of Rembrandt. Victors's picture (fig. 20) similarly features a winged, gesturing figure in white, positioned in profile on the right-hand side of the composition, although it more closely approaches the majesty and luminosity of Rembrandt's invention.[65] An especially strict Calvinist, Victors never produced a work with an image of God the Father or even Christ. His *Abraham Entertaining the Angels* suggests that he did, however, view light as an acceptable way of indicating the Lord's presence.

An autograph painting by Bol from the 1660s combines elements both from Rembrandt's painting and from his etched version of the scene (fig. 21).[66] While he portrays all three guests as winged angels, one of whom is in white, he composes the scene so that a cloaked Sarah, leaning against the open door, stands directly behind the group of divine visitors and looks at the speaking figure, as in his former master's 1656 etching. Curiously, he positions the angel who gracefully stands with his back to the viewer in such a way that one of his companions is obscured—perhaps an indication of Bol's own exploration of the complexities of sight and faith.

Rembrandt's last pupil, Aert de Gelder (1645–1727), also referred to both his master's painted and his etched versions. De Gelder's painting of the 1680s (fig. 22) portrays one of Abraham's visitors as an older bearded

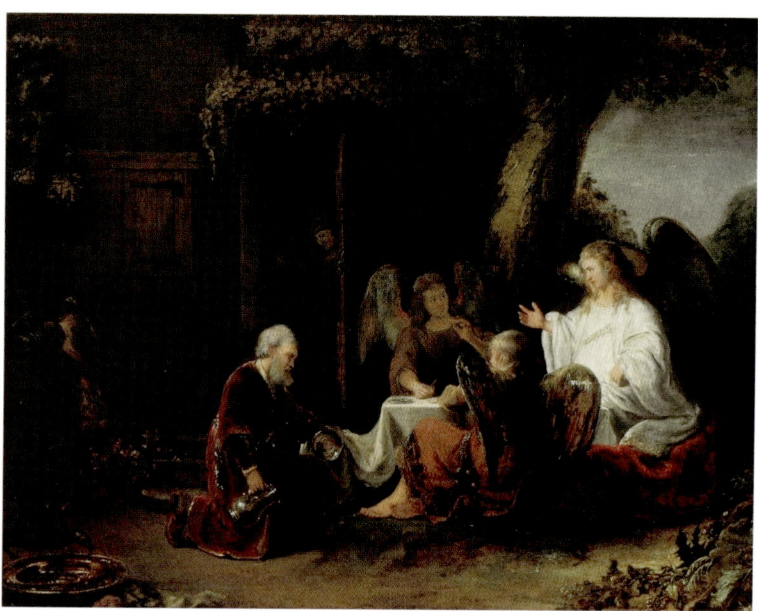

Fig. 19 Attributed to Ferdinand Bol (1616–1680), *Abraham Entertaining the Angels*, ca. 1650. Oil on canvas, 22 ¼ × 28 ½ inches (56.6 × 72.4 cm). Private collection

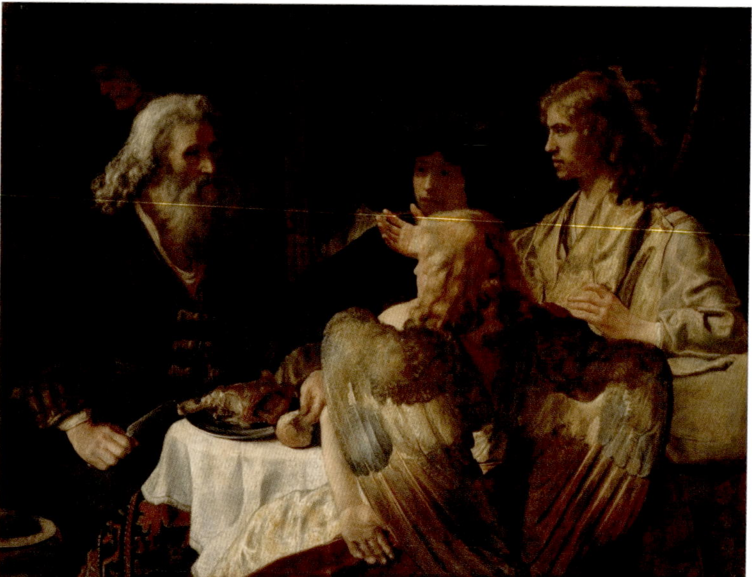

Fig. 20 Attributed to Jan Victors (1619–1676), *Abraham Entertaining the Angels*, later 1640s(?). Oil on canvas, 47 ⅝ × 63 ¾ inches (121 × 162 cm). State Hermitage Museum, St. Petersburg

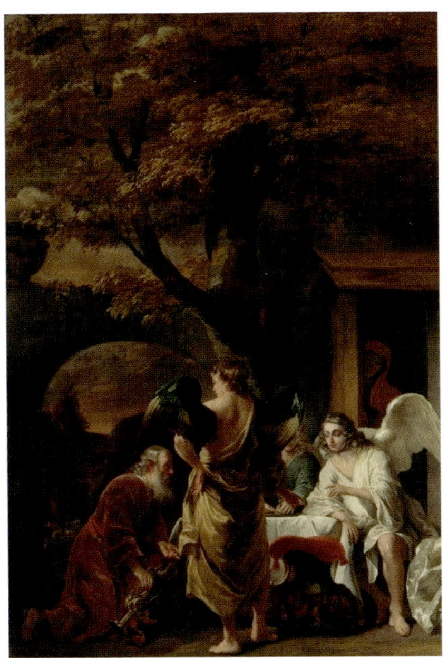

Fig. 21 Ferdinand Bol (1616–1680), *Abraham Entertaining the Angels*, 1660–63. Oil on canvas, 159 1/16 × 111 1/4 inches (404 × 282.5 cm). Rijksmuseum, Amsterdam; Gift of the Royaards Family, Utrecht

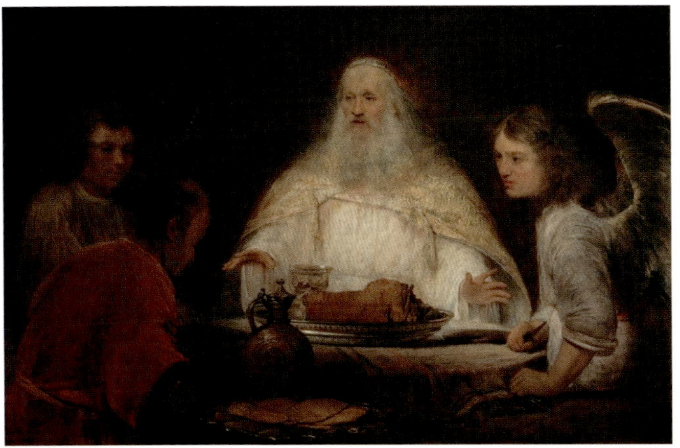

Fig. 22 Aert de Gelder (1645–1727), *Abraham Entertaining the Angels*, ca. 1680–85. Oil on canvas, 43 11/16 × 68 1/2 inches (111 × 174 cm). Museum Boijmans Van Beuningen, Rotterdam

man who, like the figure in Rembrandt's 1656 etching, is immediately identifiable as the Lord but who also possesses some of the luminosity of the winged figure in the 1646 painting.

It has long been assumed that De Gelder was the only artist to follow the corporeal representation of God in Rembrandt's print. However, Nicolaes Maes (1634–1693), who trained with Rembrandt sometime between 1646 and 1653, produced two drawings depicting the moment of Genesis 18 in which the three strangers first arrive, and Abraham, in

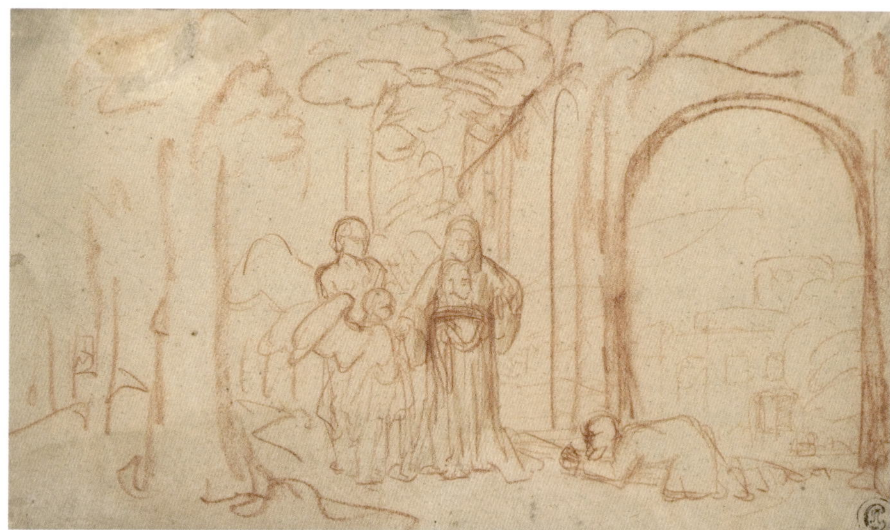

Fig. 23 Nicolaes Maes (1634–1693), *Abraham Prostrated before the Lord and the Two Angels*, ca. 1656. Red chalk on paper, 6 11⁄16 × 11 ½ inches (17 × 29.3 cm). The British Museum, London

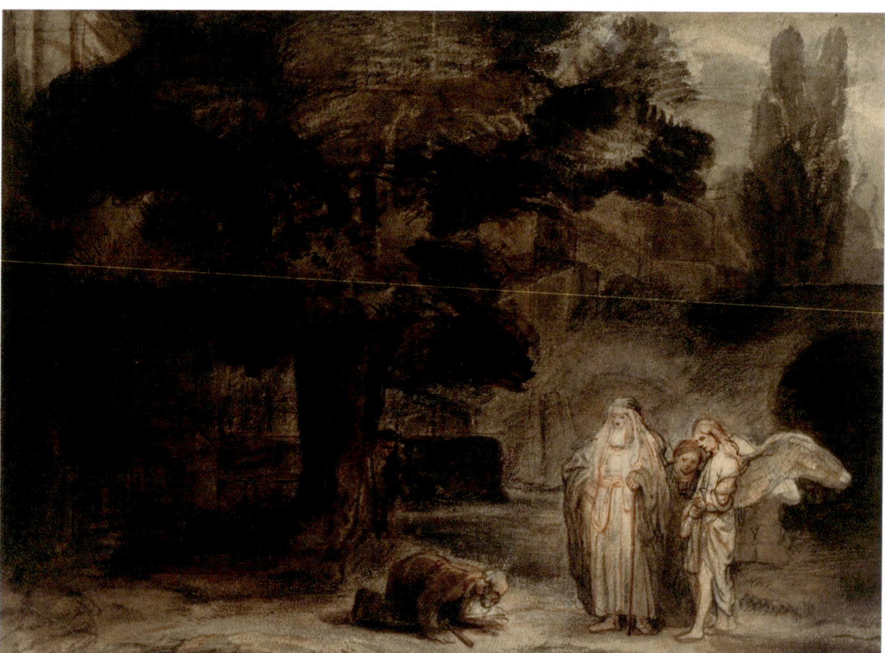

Fig. 24 Nicolaes Maes (1634–1693), *Abraham Prostrated before the Lord and the Two Angels*, ca. 1656. Pen and brown ink with red and black chalk and brown and gray wash on paper, 9 1⁄16 × 12 13⁄16 inches (23.1 × 32.6 cm). The British Museum, London

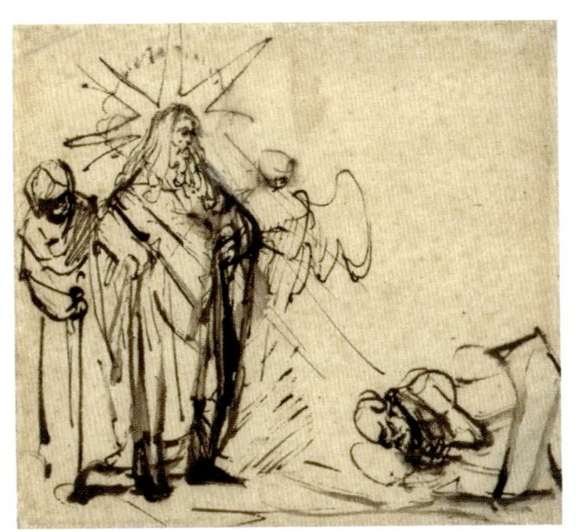

Fig. 25 Ferdinand Bol (1616–1680), *Abraham Meeting the Lord and Two Angels*, after 1646. Pen and ink on paper, 5 11⁄16 × 6 ¼ inches (14.5 × 15.9 cm). Rijksprentenkabinet, Rijksmuseum, Amsterdam; Gift of C. Hofstede de Groot, The Hague

accordance with the biblical text, bows to the ground (see cat. 9). In a compositional study in red chalk (fig. 23), we can see Maes working out one of the three guests, first drawing a small figure, then enlarging him, turning him from profile to frontal view, and changing his costume—the results of which become clear in a more developed drawing by the artist of the same scene in reverse (fig. 24), where this figure closely resembles the figure of God in Rembrandt's etching.[67]

Another work by Bol, a drawing believed to date from the late 1640s or after and surely inspired by Rembrandt's 1646 painting, may, in turn, have played a role in stimulating Rembrandt's 1656 etching. This sheet, which also presents the moment of Genesis 18 in which the three visitors first arrive (fig. 25),[68] appears to be the first depiction of Genesis 18 to feature a majestic bearded figure that is immediately recognizable as the Lord. Rembrandt undoubtedly discussed his ongoing interest in the appearance and perception of the divine with his students before and after they left his studio, and learned as well from their depictions of Genesis 18.

THINGS NOT SEEN

About 1659, Rembrandt made a final image of Abraham, again revisiting the subject of Isaac's sacrifice. In his half-length painting of the apostle Paul (fig. 26), he incorporates a representation of the scene, very similar to his own etching from 1655 (see cat. 7), in the form of a barely perceptible framed roundel hanging in the background at upper left. With this image within an image, Rembrandt alludes to Paul's epistle to the Hebrews, in which he emphasizes Abraham's willingness to sacrifice Isaac as an example of unshakable faith in God.[69] The apostle begins this passage with the remark: "Now faith is the substance of things hoped for, the evidence of things not seen."[70] For Rembrandt, an artist who frequently engaged with themes of blindness and voyeurism, these words offered the ultimate artistic challenge—to represent in visual form that which cannot be seen. Through his sustained engagement with the Abraham narrative and its confrontations between the material and immaterial, the visible and invisible, the artist took on this challenge again and again. Between Calvinist exegesis and Cartesian philosophy, he found his own visual articulation of the non-visual experience of revelation.

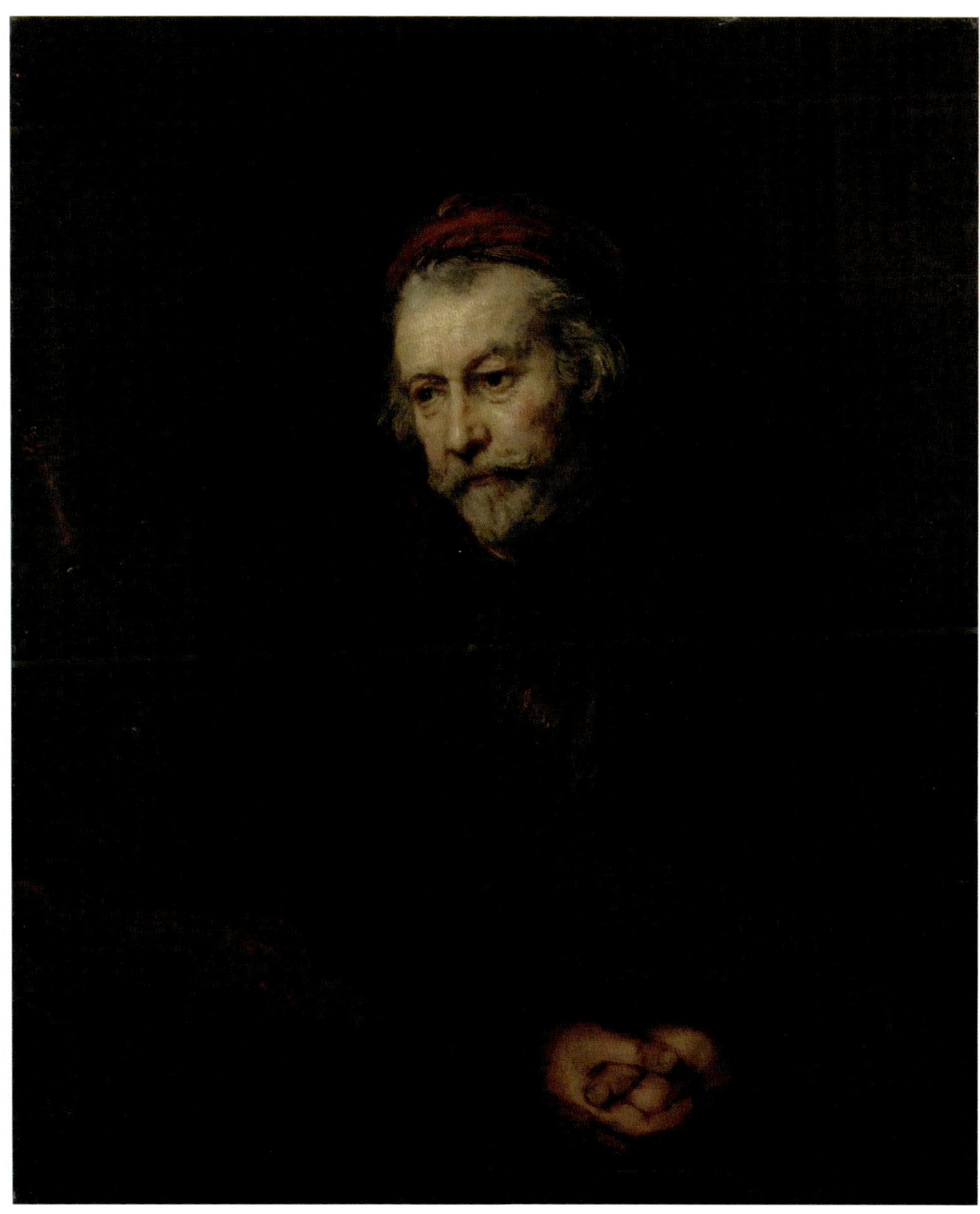

Fig. 26 Rembrandt, *St. Paul*, probably 1659. Oil on canvas, 40 ⅛ × 33 ¹¹⁄₁₆ inches (102 × 85.5 cm). The National Gallery, London; Bequeathed by Lord Colborne, 1854

Notes

1 Perlove 1989; Perlove and Silver 2009, 76–92.
2 See esp. Perlove and Silver 2009, the most comprehensive study of Rembrandt's religious imagery to date, and Perlove 1989, which focuses on Rembrandt's depictions of Abraham. The Dutch Reformed Church was the de facto official religious institution of the Dutch Republic. Rembrandt was not a member, but he baptized and buried family members in the Church and had no other documented religious affiliations.
3 Blankert in Washington/Detroit/Amsterdam 1980, 48–49. See also Blankert 1982, 34–36.
4 For a discussion of this phrase and its meaning, see Van de Wetering 2010, 133–35.
5 Perlove and Silver 2009, esp. 7–9.
6 Sellin 2006, 29.
7 Ibid., 101.
8 Rembrandt treated Hagar's encounter with the angel in a drawing of the 1650s (Hamburger Kunsthalle; Benesch 1954–57, 5: no. 904, 265).
9 Benesch 1954–57, 2: 102, no. 447.
10 Perlove (1989, 16) and Perlove and Silver (2009, 86) offer an alternative reading of Sarah's laughter as one of spiritual rejoicing. They also discuss the possibility that Rembrandt's print was in demand among Jewish collectors. Samuel D'Orta, an artist and member of Amsterdam's Jewish community, purchased the copper plate for this etching, presumably with the intention of printing impressions for sale (see De Groot 1976, 71–77; Strauss and Van der Meulen 1979, 145–46; Schwartz 1985, 194).
11 On the significance of Abraham's placement on the threshold, see Kuretsky 1997, 63; on his outstretched arms, see Sellin 2006, 110. Rembrandt reprised this banishment scene in a drawing from the 1650s (Rijksmuseum, Amsterdam; Benesch 1954–57, 5: 267–68, no. 916). There, Ishmael also faces away from the viewer, while Abraham's outstretched hand seems to make contact with the boy's head in a gesture of blessing, as in Lastman's painting.
12 Tümpel 1984, 189; Jeroense and A. Tümpel in Amsterdam 1996–97, 79; Perlove and Silver 2009, 87–88. On Rembrandt's related uses of Josephus, see also Golahny 2003, 164–79.
13 See Held's discussion of this work in his essay of 1970 about Rembrandt and the spoken word in Held 1991, esp. 169, along with Perlove and Silver 2009, 87–88.
14 Held 1991, 169. For another discussion of the depiction of such verbal exchanges in Dutch art, see Alpers 1983, 207–20.
15 Jordan (1893, 301n. 4) reidentified this etching as *Jacob Caressing Benjamin*, in view of another prominent father-and-son relationship in Genesis. Most scholars continued to refer to it as *Abraham Caressing Isaac* until Tümpel (1968, 113–15) supported Jordan's identification largely on the basis of the iconographic tradition and the image's resemblance to a figural group in another work by Rembrandt, in which Jacob indeed sits with his arms around the young Benjamin. Van der Coelen (in Amsterdam 1996–97, 96–97), Ackley (in Boston/Chicago 2003–4, 131), Golahny (2003, 174), and Perlove and Silver (2009, 100) follow Tümpel, while Franits (1981/82), Nieuwstraten (1998, 166), and Hinterding (2008, 74–75) present compelling arguments in favor of the Abraham identification. See also New Hollstein 2013, 2: 20–21, no. 165, where the print is catalogued as *Abraham Caressing Isaac*.
16 Perlove 1989, 16. Perlove also notes the connection to traditional imagery of the Christ Child holding an apple and the resemblance of the figural arrangement to that of the Virgin and Christ Child in Raphael's *La Belle Jardinière* (Louvre, Paris).
17 In the original Dutch: "vaeder Abraham speelend met sijn soon." See De Hoop Scheffer and Boon 1971, 8; and Hinterding 2008, 75.
18 Talmud, Bava Metzia 86b. See also Miller, W., 1984, 8–42, esp. 16–19, 36–38.
19 On this literature, see Kloos 2011, 4–7, 13–97, and Erffa 1995, 2: 99–101.
20 Kloos 2011, 4–7.
21 Augustine, *Contra Maximinum Arrianum* 2.26.5–7. Discussed in Kloos 2011, 8, 17–73.
22 Ibid., 171–73.
23 The earliest extant depiction of the episode is a fourth-century wall painting in the Via Latina catacomb in Rome. It shows the three visitors without any markers of divinity, although it should be noted that angels with wings began to appear in Christian art only in the fourth century. A rare visual treatment of the subject in a Jewish context appears in one of the fifth-century floor mosaics of the synagogue at Sepphoris; unfortunately, damage obscures the representation of the three visitors (see Weiss 2005, 153–61).
24 On the program of the Santa Maria Maggiore mosaics, see Spain 1968.
25 For a list of literature on the iconography of this scene, see Erffa 1995, 2: 101–2. My deepest thanks to Charlotte Rulkens for her work in tracing the pictorial tradition from the medieval period to the eighteenth century.
26 I:XVIII:9. Translated in Calvin 1948, 472. Perlove and Silver (2009, 76) discuss this passage in relation to Rembrandt's painting.
27 For a partial English translation of this note, see Van de Wetering 2010, 426n. 22.
28 Even in 1700, Willem Goeree, a writer on religion and on art, still had reason to discuss the question of Abraham's perception of the strangers (Goeree 1700, 266–68). On Goeree, see Van de Lindt 2009.
29 Van de Kamp (1991, 29) writes that the choice to differentiate one of the three figures, in line with Calvin, begins to occur in the second quarter of the seventeenth century but cites nothing earlier than Rembrandt's painting. There does exist, however, a depiction of the scene attributed to Lambert Jacobsz (1598–1636) and assigned a date of 1628 (Frees Museum, Leeuwarden) that portrays three travelers, none with wings, one of whom is in white. Regarding a painting attributed to Jan

Victors and traditionally dated to the 1630s, see my discussion below.

30 Wittrock 1974 and Tümpel 1969, 153.

31 For a similar discussion, focused on Rembrandt's New Testament imagery, see Keyes 2011–12, esp. 4–14. For a different interpretation of this shift in Rembrandt's art, see Sluijter 2006, 105–9, 137–38, and Sluijter 2010, 285–305.

32 For a seminal discussion that relates these advances to seventeenth-century Dutch art, see Alpers 1983, 26–81.

33 Sluijter 2000, 9–10. See also Clark 2007.

34 Descartes 1637, which was accompanied by an essay dedicated to optics, and Descartes 1641. So rapidly were Descartes's ideas taken up in academic circles in the Dutch Republic that there were already calls to ban the teaching of Cartesian ideas at some of its universities by the early 1640s. See Verbeek 1992; Israel 2002, 24–29; and Frijhoff and Spies 2004, 281–320.

35 Descartes 1637, 4: 37. Translated in Descartes 2006, 109.

36 For a similar discussion, see Ketelsen 2004, 15.

37 Golahny 2003, 174.

38 Perlove and Silver (2009, 91) also observe that Abraham's eyes are open.

39 Translated and discussed in ibid., 90.

40 Perlove and Silver (2009, 90) note that the Dutch States Bible identifies this angel as the Son of God. See also Tümpel (in Paris 2007, 49), who notes that Josephus attributes this intervention to God himself.

41 Smith 1985, 296.

42 Roscam Abbing (1993, 28–33), offered the first dedicated discussion of Rembrandt's choice to depict the Lord in this image.

43 Royalton-Kisch 1992, 141–44. See also Duda 1997, 41–43.

44 See Sarre 1904; Lunsingh Scheurleer 1980; Courtright 1996; Filipczak 2007–8; and Forberg 2015.

45 Royalton-Kisch 1992, 141–44.

46 There was at least some knowledge of Islam in the Dutch Republic. Dutch translations of the Qu'ran appeared in the 1640s and 1650s, while trade between the Republic and the Mughal Empire and Middle East would have offered many other sources of information about the religion. It may also be noteworthy that in Islamic tradition, Ishmael is an ancestor of Mohammed. In his history of the Jews, Flavius Josephus himself identified Ishmael as the ancestor of an Arab nation (Book I, chapter 12).

47 See Filipczak 2007–8, 178–84.

48 Heenk (1996, 48–50) explains that in the seventeenth century, the copper plate made its way into the collection of an artist—now identified as a follower of the Flemish painter Peeter Gysels (1621–1690)—who painted a river landscape on the back of it. As a result, the etched surface on the other side was not discovered until 1996. See also Wheelock 2005, 117–19.

49 Ishmael does appear in a few later treatments of the subject, for example, a painting from the 1660s by Giovanni Andrea de' Ferrari (Saint Louis Art Museum) and an eighteenth-century Dutch print by Jacob de Later after Gerard Hoet. An earlier, ambiguous case is Ludovico Carracci's version of the scene, in which Sarah appears in the background at left and another figure, possibly Ishmael, stands by the tree at center (Pinacoteca Nazionale di Bologna).

50 Perlove 1994–96, 88–90, and Perlove and Silver 2009, 81–82.

51 Felgenhauer 1655, 11. Translated in Zell 2002, 182.

52 Zell 2002, 182. Perlove (1994–96, 88–91) had also linked Rembrandt's etching of 1656, and other works, with the millenarian expectations of the decade, but with an understanding of Ishmael as ignoring the Lord's divine announcement. See also Perlove and Silver 2009, 82.

53 On these illustrations for Menasseh ben Israel's *Piedra gloriosa* of 1655, see especially Van de Waal 1954–55; Zell 2002, 72–98; Nadler 2003, 132–41; Paris 2007, 318–21; Hinterding 2008, 80–86; Perlove and Silver 2009, 134–37; and New Hollstein 2013, 2: 248–51. For revisionist arguments that Menasseh did not commission these illustrations from Rembrandt, see Dubiez 1992 and Amsterdam 2006–7, 24–26. In my view, the more likely scenario is that Menasseh did commission Rembrandt's etchings after he printed the text, if only for a few designated copies of the book, intended for specific readers, and that he surely discussed their content with the artist. The fact that the reprintings of the book include close copies of Rembrandt's etchings also supports this.

54 Menasseh ben Israel 1655, 60. Translated and discussed in Zell 2002, 184.

55 First observed by David de Witt, as reported in Van de Wetering 2010, 419.

56 For similar discussions of Abraham's downward gaze in relation to questions of divine presence and invisibility, see Ketelsen 2004, 15–16, and Paris 2007, 264.

57 The angels' distinctive features have encouraged proposals that they are portraits: Winternitz 1977, 104–6; Perlove 1994–96, 88–90; and Zell 2002, 186–87.

58 See Perlove 1989, 13.

59 Veldman (2001, 65–66) notes the light stippling with which De Passe distinguishes the figure, "making it less objectionable to orthodox Protestants, who disapproved of depicting God in human form."

60 In many cases, as with Cornelis Cort's engraving after Maarten van Heemskerck, printmakers and print publishers took existing plates that featured images of God and simply modified them or created copies in which the offending motif was removed. See Veldman 1999, 417–18, and Tanis 1999, 377–80.

61 Paris 2007, 264. See also note 53 above. Among the copies that appear in subsequent printings

of Menasseh's book, *Daniel's Vision of the Four Beasts* omits the figure of God.

62 Ketelsen 2004, 14–16.

63 In addition to the examples discussed in this essay, there are two paintings by Gerbrand van den Eeckhout (State Hermitage Museum, St. Petersburg, and Rembrandthuis, Amsterdam) and various drawings attributed to Samuel van Hoogstraten (Kupferstichkabinett, Berlin, Kupferstich-Kabinett, Dresden, and private collection); Barent Fabritius (sold Sotheby's London, July 11, 2001); Nicolaes Maes (Teylers Museum, Haarlem, and Yale University Art Gallery, New Haven); and Justus de Gelder (Teylers Museum, Haarlem).

64 On the early provenance of Rembrandt's painting and Bol's probable ownership of it, see Van de Wetering 2010, 422–23, 425–26.

65 Sumowski (1983, IV: 2596, no. 1722) dated this work to the 1630s based on the then widely held presumption that Victors trained with Rembrandt in that decade (see also Berlin/Amsterdam/London 1991–92, 334–37, cat. no. 67). Sluijter (2015, 363–64) has demonstrated that Victors was never a member of Rembrandt's studio.

66 On this painting and the decorative cycle to which it originally belonged, see Van Eikema Hommes 2012.

67 The British Museum dates the more developed sheet to about 1650 and the red-chalk drawing to about 1665, but, given the relationship of the two figures in these works, it is more likely that the red-chalk drawing preceded the other, although the dates of both are uncertain.

68 Leja 2013. Leja also discusses a related sheet in the Albertina, Vienna, attributing it to Bol's workshop.

69 MacLaren 1960, 319–20. See discussions in Smith 1985, 294–95, and Perlove and Silver 2009, 12–14.

70 Hebrews 11:1.

Bibliography

Alpers 1983
Alpers, Svetlana. *The Art of Describing: Dutch Art in the Seventeenth Century*. Chicago: University of Chicago Press, 1983.

Alpers 1988
Alpers, Svetlana. *Rembrandt's Enterprise: The Studio and Market*. Chicago: University of Chicago Press, 1988.

Amsterdam 1996–97
Van der Coelen, Peter, et al. *Patriarchs, Angels & Prophets: The Old Testament in Netherlandish Printmaking from Lucas van Leyden to Rembrandt*. Exh. cat. Amsterdam (Rembrandthuis), 1996–97.

Amsterdam 2006–7
Alexander-Knotter, Mirjam, et al. *The "Jewish" Rembrandt: The Myth Unravelled*. Exh. cat. Amsterdam (Jewish Historical Museum), 2006–7.

Amsterdam/Berlin 2006
Van de Wetering, Ernst, et al. *Rembrandt: Quest of a Genius*. Exh. cat. Amsterdam (Rembrandthuis) and Berlin (Gemäldegalerie, Staatliche Museen zu Berlin), 2006.

Amsterdam/Jerusalem 1991
Tümpel, Christian, et al. *Het Oude Testament in de schilderkunst van de Gouden Eeuw*. Exh. cat. Amsterdam (Jewish Historical Museum) and Jerusalem (Israel Museum), 1991.

Auerbach 2008
Auerbach, Elissa. "Taking Mary's Pulse: Cartesianism and Modernity in Rembrandt's 'The Death of the Virgin.'" In *Power and Image in Early Modern Europe*, edited by Jessica Goethals, et al. Newcastle upon Tyne: Cambridge Scholars Publishing, 2008.

Bakhos 2014
Bakhos, Carol. *The Family of Abraham: Jewish, Christian, and Muslim Interpretations*. Cambridge, Massachusetts: Harvard University Press, 2014.

Benesch 1954–57
Benesch, Otto. *The Drawings of Rembrandt*. 6 vols. London: Phaidon Press, 1954–57.

Berlin 2014
Beyer, Vera, et al. *Joseph und Zulaikha: Beziehungsgeschichten zwischen Indien, Persien und Europa*. Exh. cat. Berlin (Staatliche Museen zu Berlin), 2014.

Berlin/Amsterdam/London 1991–92
Brown, Christopher, et al. *Rembrandt: The Master and His Workshop*. 2 vols. Exh. cat. Berlin (Altes Museum, Staatliche Museen zu Berlin), Amsterdam (Rijksmuseum), and London (National Gallery), 1991–92.

Blankert 1982
Blankert, Albert. *Ferdinand Bol (1616–1680): Rembrandt's Pupil*. Doornspijk: Davaco Publishers, 1982.

Boston/Chicago 2003–4
Ackley, Clifford S., et al. *Rembrandt's Journey: Painter, Draftsman, Etcher*. Exh. cat. Boston (Museum of Fine Arts) and Chicago (Art Institute of Chicago), 2003–4.

Bryson 1983
Bryson, Norman. *Vision and Painting: The Logic of the Gaze*. New Haven: Yale University Press, 1983.

Calvin 1948
Calvin, John. *Commentaries on the First Book of Moses, Called Genesis*, vol. 1. Translated by John King. Grand Rapids: Wm. B. Eerdmans Publishing Company, 1948. Originally published as *In primum Mosis libru[m], qui Genesis vulgo dicitur, Commentarius Iohannis Calvini* (Geneva, 1554).

Calvin 2011
Calvin, John. *The Institutes of the Christian Religion*, vol. 1. Translated and edited by Henry Beveridge. Seattle: Pacific Publishing Studio, 2011. Originally published as *Christianae religionis institutio* (Basel, 1536).

Carriero 2009
Carriero, John Peter. *Between Two Worlds: A Reading of Descartes's Meditations*. Princeton: Princeton University Press, 2009.

Cats 1862
Cats, Jacob. *Alle de werken*. 2 vols. Edited by J. van Vloten. Zwolle: De Erven J. J. Tijl, 1862.

Clark 2007
Clark, Stuart. *Vanities of the Eye: Vision in Early Modern European Culture*. Oxford: Oxford University Press, 2007.

Van der Coelen 1997
Van der Coelen, Peter. "De statenbijbel en de prentkunst. Over een 'liefhebber' en een 'yvrigh kerkelijk man.'" *Transparent* 8 (1997): 30–36.

Courtright 1996
Courtright, Nicola. "Origins and Meanings of Rembrandt's Late Drawing Style." *The Art Bulletin* 78, no. 3 (Sept. 1996): 485–510.

Crenshaw 2006
Crenshaw, Paul. *Rembrandt's Bankruptcy: The Artist, His Patrons, and the Art Market in Seventeenth-Century Netherlands*. Cambridge: Cambridge University Press, 2006.

Dearborn 1989
Perlove, Shelley, et al. *Impressions of Faith: Rembrandt's Biblical Etchings*. Exh. cat. Dearborn (University of Michigan-Dearborn, Mardigian Library), 1989.

Dearborn 2010
Perlove, Shelley, et al. *Pursuit of Faith: Etchings by Rembrandt from the Thrivent Financial Collection of Religious Art*. Exh. cat. Dearborn (Alfred Berkowitz Gallery of the University of Michigan-Dearborn), 2010.

Descartes 1637
Descartes, René. *Discours de la méthode pour bien conduire sa raison & chercher la verité dans les sciences: plus la dioptrique, les météores, et la géométrie, qui sont des essais de cete méthode*. Leiden: I. Maire, 1637.

Descartes 1641
Descartes, René. *Meditationes de prima philosophia: in qua Dei existentia et anima immortalitas demonstratur*. Paris: M. Soly, 1641.

Descartes 2006
Descartes, René. *A Discourse on the Method of Correctly Conducting One's Reason and Seeking Truth in the Sciences*. Translated and with an introduction and notes by Ian Maclean. Oxford: Oxford University Press, 2006.

Descartes 2012
Descartes, René. *Meditations on First Philosophy: With Selections from the Objections and Replies: A Latin-English Edition*. Translated and edited by John Cottingham. New York: Cambridge University Press, 2012.

Dittrich, Ketelsen, et al. 2004
Dittrich, Christian, Thomas Ketelsen, et al. *Rembrandt, die Dresdener Zeichnungen*. Cologne: Verlag der Buchhandlung Walter König, 2004.

Dubiez 1992
Dubiez, F. J. "Drie beeldende kunstenaars en drie rabbijnen te Amsterdam in de zeventiende eeuw." *Kroniek van het Rembrandthuis* (1992): 23–32.

Duda 1997
Duda, Dorothea. "Die Kaiserin und der Großmogul Untersuchungen zu den Miniaturen des Millionenzimmers im Schloss Schönbrunn." In *Malerei auf Papier und Pergament in den Prunkraümen des Schlosses Schönbrunn*, edited by Karin K. Troschke. Vienna: Schloss Schönbrunn Kultur- und Betriebsges, 1997.

Dudok van Heel 2006
Dudok van Heel, Sebastien Abraham Corneille. *De jonge Rembrandt onder tijdgenoten. Godsdienst en schilderkunst in Leiden en Amsterdam*. Ph.D. diss., Radboud Universiteit Nijmegen, 2006.

Van Eikema Hommes 2012
Van Eikema Hommes, Margriet. *Art and Allegiance in the Dutch Golden Age: The Ambitions of a Wealthy Widow in a Painted Chamber by Ferdinand Bol*. Amsterdam: Amsterdam University Press, 2012.

Erffa 1995
Erffa, Hans Martin von. *Ikonologie der Genesis: Die christlichen Bildthemen aus dem Alten Testament und ihre Quellen*, vol. 2. Munich and Berlin: Deutscher Kunstverlag, 1995.

Felgenhauer 1665
Felgenhauer, Paul. *Bonum Nuncium Israeli: Quod offertur Populo Israel & Iude in hisce temporibus novissimis de Messiah*. Amsterdam: Typis Georgii Trigge, 1655.

Filipczak 2007/8
Filipczak, Zirka Z. "Rembrandt and the Body Language of Mughal Miniatures." *Nederlands Kunsthistorisch Jaarboek* 58 (2007/8): 163–84.

Finney 1999
Finney, Paul Corbey, ed. *Seeing beyond the Word: Visual Arts and the Calvinist Tradition*. Cambridge: William B. Eerdmans Publishing Company, 1999.

Forberg 2015
Forberg, Corinna. *Die Rezeption Indischer Miniaturen in der europäischen Kunst des 17. und 18. Jahrhunderts*. Petersberg: Michael Imhof Verlag, 2015.

Franits 1981/82
Franits, Wayne. "On the Subject Matter of Rembrandt's Etching B. 33." *Marsyas* 21 (1981/82): 13–16.

Freedberg 1988
Freedberg, David. *Iconoclasm and Painting in the Revolt of the Netherlands 1566–1609*. New York: Garland Publishing, 1988.

Friedländer 1926
Friedländer, Max J. *Die Kunstsammlung von Pannwitz. Band I: Gemälde*. Munich: Verlag F. Bruckmann, 1926.

Frijhoff and Spies 2004
Frijhoff, Willem, and Marijke Spies. *Dutch Culture in a European Perspective, I: 1650: Hard-Won Unity*. Assen: Royal Van Gorcum; Basingstoke and New York: Palgrave Macmillan, 2004.

Goeree 1700
Goeree, Willem. *Mozaische historie der Hebreeuwse Kerke*. 4 vols. Amsterdam: Willem and David Goeree, 1700.

Golahny 2003
Golahny, Amy. *Rembrandt's Reading: The Artist's Bookshelf of Ancient Poetry and History*. Amsterdam: Amsterdam University Press, 2003.

De Groot 1976
De Groot, D. "Een archiefvondst: Rembrandt verkoopt in 1637 een koperplaat." *Jaarboek Amstelodamum* 68, nos. 1–2 (1976): 71–77.

Hamburg 2006
Sitt, Martina, ed. *Pieter Lastman: In Rembrandts Schatten*. Exh. cat. Hamburg (Hamburger Kunsthalle), 2006.

Heenk 1996
Heenk, Liesbeth. "The Discovery of an Etched Copperplate by Rembrandt." *Kroniek van het Rembrandthuis* (1996): 48–49.

Held 1991
Held, Julius S. "Rembrandt and the Spoken Word (1970)." In Julius S. Held, *Rembrandt Studies*. Princeton: Princeton University Press, 1991.

Hinterding 1995
Hinterding, Erik. *The History of Rembrandt's Copperplates: With a Catalogue of Those that Survive*. Zwolle: Waanders, 1995.

Hinterding 2004
Hinterding, Erik. "Rembrandt's Etchings of Biblical and Mythological Subjects: Associations with His Painting." In *Rembrandt and Dutch History Painting in the Seventeenth Century*, edited by Akira Kofuku. Tokyo: The National Museum of Western Art, 2004.

Hinterding 2006
Hinterding, Erik. *Rembrandt as an Etcher*. 3 vols. Ouderkerk aan den IJssel: Sound & Vision, 2006.

Hinterding 2008
Hinterding, Erik. *Rembrandt Etchings from the Frits Lugt Collection*. 2 vols. Bussum: THOTH Publishers; Paris: Fondation Custodia, 2008.

De Hoop Scheffer and Boon 1971
De Hoop Scheffer, Dieuwke, and Karel G. Boon. "De inventarislijst van Clement de Jonghe en Rembrandts etsplaten." *Kroniek van het Rembrandthuis* (1971): 1–17.

Israel 1995
Israel, Jonathan I. *The Dutch Republic: Its Rise, Its Greatness, Its Fall, 1477–1806*. Oxford and New York: Clarendon Press, 1995.

Israel 2002
Israel, Jonathan I. *Radical Enlightenment: Philosophy and the Making of Modernity, 1650–1750*. Oxford: Oxford University Press, 2002.

Jacob 2003
Jacob, Pierre. *Ways of Seeing: The Scope and Limits of Visual Cognition*. New York: Oxford University Press, 2003.

Jericke 2003
Jericke, Detlef. *Abraham in Mamre: Historische und exegetische Studien zur Region von Hebron und zu Genesis*. Leiden and Boston: Brill, 2003.

Jordan 1893
Jordan, Albrecht. "Bemerkungen zu Rembrandt's Radierungen." *Repertorium für Kunstwissenschaft* 17 (1893): 296–302.

Josephus 1574
Josephus, Flavius. *Flavij Josephi, des hochberühmten Jüdischen Geschichtschreibers Historien und Bücher*. Translated by Conrad Lautenbauch. Strasbourg: Theodosius Rihel, 1574.

Van de Kamp 1991
Van de Kamp, Netty. "Genesis: De oergeschiedenis en de verhalen van de aartsvaders." In Amsterdam/Jerusalem 1991.

Katchen 1984
Katchen, Aaron L. *Christian Hebraists and Dutch Rabbis: Seventeenth-Century Apologetics and the Study of Maimonides' Mishneh Torah*. Cambridge, Massachusetts, and London: Harvard University Press, 1984.

Ketelsen 2004
Ketelsen, Thomas. "Im Wechsel der Blicke: Beobachtungen zu Rembrandts Bilderwelten." In Dittrich, Ketelsen, et al. 2004.

Keyes 2011–12
Keyes, George S. "Perception and Belief: The Image of Christ and the Meditative Turn in Rembrandt's Religious Art." In Philadelphia/Paris/Detroit 2011–12.

Kloos 2011
Kloos, Kari. *Christ, Creation, and the Vision of God: Augustine's Transformation of Early Christian Theophany Interpretation*. Leiden and Boston: Brill, 2011.

Koch 2000
Koch, Ebba. "Netherlandish Naturalism in Imperial Mughal Painting." *Apollo* 465 (2000): 29–37.

Koerner 2004
Koerner, Joseph Leo. *The Reformation of the Image*. Chicago: University of Chicago Press, 2004.

Kuretsky 1997
Kuretsky, Susan Donahue. "Rembrandt at the Threshold." In *Rembrandt, Rubens, and the Art of Their Time: Recent Perspectives*, edited by Roland E. Fleischer and Susan Claire Scott. University Park: Pennsylvania State University, 1997.

Laarmann 2011
Laarmann, Frauke. "Abraham and the Angels." In *Aemulatio: Imitation, Emulation and Invention in Netherlandish Art from 1500 to 1800: Essays in Honor of Eric Jan Sluijter*, edited by Anton W. A. Boschloo et al. Zwolle: Waanders, 2011.

Landsberger 1946
Landsberger, Franz. *Rembrandt, the Jews and the Bible*. Translated by Felix N. Gerson. Philadelphia: The Jewish Publication Society of America, 1946.

Leja 2013
Leja, Jan L. "Abraham Meeting the Lord and Two Angels: Making the Case for Ferdinand Bol and Workshop." *Journal of the Historians of Netherlandish Art* 5, no. 2 (summer 2013): DOI:10.5092/jhna.2013.5.2.13.

Letellier 1995
Letellier, Robert Ignatius. *Day in Mamre, Night in Sodom: Abraham and Lot in Genesis 18 and 19*. Leiden and New York: E. J. Brill, 1995.

Levenson 2012
Levenson, Jon D. *Inheriting Abraham: The Legacy of the Patriarch in Judaism, Christianity, and Islam*. Princeton and Oxford: Princeton University Press, 2012.

Van de Lindt 2009
Van de Lindt, Adriana. "Willem Goeree (1635–1711): Un Amateur entre art et lumières radicales." In *L'Histoire de l'histoire de l'art septentrional au XVIIe siècle*, edited by Michèle-Caroline Heck. Turnhout: Brepols, 2009.

London/Amsterdam 2014–15
Bikker, Jonathan, et al. *Rembrandt: The Late Works*. Exh. cat. London (National Gallery) and Amsterdam (Rijksmuseum), 2014–15.

Lunsingh Scheurleer 1980
Lunsingh Scheurleer, Pauline. "Mogol-miniaturen door Rembrandt nagetekend." *Kroniek van het Rembrandthuis* (1980): 10–40.

Machamer and McGuire 2009
Machamer, Peter K., and J. E. McGuire. *Descartes's Changing Mind.* Princeton: Princeton University Press, 2009.

MacLaren 1960
MacLaren, Neil. *The Dutch School.* London: National Gallery, 1960.

Manuth 1993–94
Manuth, Volker. "Denomination and Iconography: The Choice of Subject Matter in the Biblical Painting of the Rembrandt Circle." *Simiolus* 22, no. 4 (1993–94): 235–52.

Marshall and Walsham 2006
Marshall, Peter, and Alexandra Walsham. *Angels in the Early Modern World.* Cambridge and New York: Cambridge University Press, 2006.

Menasseh ben Israel 1655
Menasseh ben Israel. *Piedra gloriosa o de la Estatua de Nebuchadnesar con muchas y diversas authoridades de la S.S. y antiguos sabios.* Amsterdam, 1655.

Miller, D., 1985
Miller, Debra. "Jan Victors (1619–76)." Ph.D. diss., University of Delaware, 1985.

Miller, W., 1984
Miller, William T. *Mysterious Encounters at Mamre and Jabbok.* Chico, California: Scholars Press, 1984.

Milwaukee 1976
Bader, Alfred. *The Bible through Dutch Eyes: From Genesis through the Apocrypha.* Exh. cat. Milwaukee (Milwaukee Art Center), 1976.

Mochizuki 2008
Mochizuki, Mia M. *The Netherlandish Image after Iconoclasm, 1566–1672: Material Religion in the Dutch Golden Age.* Aldershot and Burlington, Vermont: Ashgate, 2008.

Von Moltke 1994
Von Moltke, J. W. *Arent de Gelder. Dordrecht 1645–1727.* Doornspijk: Davaco Publishers, 1994.

Müller 2015
Müller, Jürgen. *Der sokratische Künstler: Studien zu Rembrandts Nachtwachte.* Leiden: Brill, 2015.

Nadler 2003
Nadler, Steven. *Rembrandt's Jews.* Chicago: University of Chicago Press, 2003.

New Hollstein 2013
The New Hollstein. Dutch & Flemish Etchings, Engravings and Woodcuts 1450–1700: Rembrandt. 7 vols. Compiled by Erik Hinterding and Jaco Rutgers. Edited by Ger Luijten. Ouderkerk aan den IJssel: Sound & Vision; Amsterdam: Rijksprentenkabinet, Rijksmuseum, 2013.

New York/Chicago 1988
O'Neill, John P., ed. *Dutch and Flemish Paintings from the Hermitage.* Exh. cat. New York (Metropolitan Museum of Art) and Chicago (Art Institute of Chicago), 1988.

Nieuwstraten 1998
Nieuwstraten, J. "Het werkelijke onderwerp van Aert de Gelders 'Heilige Familie' te Berlijn." *Oud Holland* 112, nos. 2/3 (1998): 157–68.

Paris 2007
Sigal-Klagsbald, Laurence, Alexis Merle du Bourg, et al. *Rembrandt et la Nouvelle Jérusalem: Juifs et chrétiens à Amsterdam au siècle d'or.* Exh. cat. Paris (Musée d'art et d'histoire du Judaïsme), 2007.

Perlove 1989
Perlove, Shelley Karen. "Visual Exegesis: The Calvinist Context for Rembrandt's Etchings of the Life of Abraham." In Dearborn 1989.

Perlove 1994–96
Perlove, Shelley. "Awaiting the Messiah: Christians, Jews, and Muslims in the Late Work of Rembrandt." *Bulletin of the University of Michigan Museums of Art and Archaeology* 11 (1994–96): 84–113.

Perlove and Silver 2009
Perlove, Shelley, and Larry Silver. *Rembrandt's Faith: Church and Temple in the Dutch Golden Age.* University Park: Pennsylvania State University Press, 2009.

Philadelphia/Paris/Detroit 2011–12
Dewitt, Lloyd, et al. *Rembrandt and the Face of Jesus.* Exh. cat. Philadelphia (Philadelphia Museum of Art), Paris (Musée du Louvre), and Detroit (Detroit Institute of Arts), 2011–12.

Raupp 1994
Raupp, Hans-Joachim. "Rembrandts Radierungen mit biblischen Themen 1640–1650 und das 'Hundertguldenblatt.'" *Zeitschrift für Kunstgeschichte* 57, no. 3 (1994): 403–20.

Robinson 1989
Robinson, William. "Nicolaes Maes as a Draughtsman." *Master Drawings* 27, no. 2 (1989): 146–62.

Robinson 1996
Robinson, William. "The Early Works of Nicolaes Maes 1653 to 1661." Ph.D. diss., Harvard University, 1996.

Roscam Abbing 1993
Roscam Abbing, Michiel. "Abraham onthaalt de Heer en twee engelen. Opmerkingen over de titel van de Rembrandt-ets B. 29." *Kroniek van het Rembrandthuis* (1993): 28–33.

Roy 1992
Roy, Alain. *Gérard de Lairesse (1640–1711).* Paris: Association pour la diffusion de l'Histoire de l'Art, 1992.

Royalton-Kisch 1992
Royalton-Kisch, Martin. *Drawings by Rembrandt and His Circle in the British Museum.* London: British Museum Press, 1992.

Sarre 1904
Sarre, Friedrich. "Rembrandts Zeichnungen nach Indisch-islamischen Miniaturen." *Jahrbuch der Königlich Preussischen Kunstsammlungen* 25, no. 3 (1904): 143–58.

Schama 1999
Schama, Simon. *Rembrandt's Eyes*. New York: Alfred A. Knopf, 1999.

Schatborn 1985
Schatborn, Peter. *Catalogus van de Nederlandse tekeningen in het Rijksprentenkabinet, Rijksmuseum, Amsterdam, IV: Tekeningen van Rembrandt, zijn onbekende leerlingen en navolgers*. The Hague, 1985.

Schwartz 1985
Schwartz, Gary. *Rembrandt: His Life, His Paintings*. New York: Viking, 1985.

Schwartz 2006
Schwartz, Gary. *The Rembrandt Book*. New York: Abrams, 2006.

Seifert 2011
Seifert, Christian Tico. *Pieter Lastman: Studien zu Leben und Werk*. Petersberg: Michael Imhof Verlag, 2011.

Sellin 2006
Sellin, Christine Petra. *Fractured Families and Rebel Maidservants: The Biblical Hagar in Seventeenth-Century Dutch Art and Literature*. New York: Continuum, 2006.

Sluijter 2000
Sluijter, Eric Jan. *Seductress of Sight: Studies in Dutch Art of the Golden Age*. Zwolle: Waanders, 2000.

Sluijter 2006
Sluijter, Eric Jan. *Rembrandt and the Female Nude*. Amsterdam: Amsterdam University Press, 2006.

Sluijter 2010
Sluijter, Eric Jan. "Rembrandt's Portrayal of the Passions and Vondel's 'staetveranderinge.'" *Nederlands Kunsthistorisch Jaarboek* 60 (2010): 283–301.

Sluijter 2015
Sluijter, Eric Jan. *Rembrandt's Rivals: History Painting in Amsterdam, 1630–1650*. Amsterdam: John Benjamins, 2015.

Smith 1985
Smith, David R. "Towards a Protestant Aesthetics: Rembrandt's 1655 *Sacrifice of Isaac*." *Art History* 8, no. 3 (Sept. 1985): 290–302.

Solomons 1906
Solomons, Israel. "The Second Series of Illustrations for the Piedra Gloriosa of Manasseh ben Israel." *The Jewish Chronicle* (July 27, 1906): 31.

Spain 1968
Spain, Suzanne. "The Program of the Fifth-Century Mosaics of Santa Maria Maggiore." Ph.D. diss., New York University, 1968.

Strauss and Van der Meulen 1979
Strauss, Walter R., and Marjon van der Meulen. *The Rembrandt Documents*. New York: Abaris Books, 1979.

Stronks 2011
Stronks, Els. *Negotiating Differences: Word, Image and Religion in the Dutch Republic*. Leiden and Boston: Brill, 2011.

Sumowski 1979–92
Sumowski, Werner. *The Drawings of the Rembrandt School*. 10 vols. New York: Abaris Books, 1979–92.

Sumowski 1983
Sumowski, Werner. *Gemälde der Rembrandt-Schüler*. 6 vols. Landau: Edition PVA, 1983.

Tanis 1999
Tanis, James R. "Netherlandish Reformed Traditions in the Graphic Arts, 1550–1630." In Finney 1999.

Tümpel 1968
Tümpel, Christian. "Ikonographische Beiträge zu Rembrandt. Zur Deutung und Interpretation seiner Historien (I)." *Jahrbuch der Hamburger Kunstsammlungen* 13 (1968): 95–126.

Tümpel 1969
Tümpel, Christian. "Studien zur Ikonographie der Historien Rembrandts." *Nederlands Kunsthistorisch Jaarboek* 20 (1969): 107–98.

Tümpel 1970
Tümpel, Christian. *Rembrandt legt die Bibel aus: Zeichnungen und Radierungen aus dem Kupferstichkabinett der Staatlichen Museen Preussischer Kulturbesitz Berlin*. Berlin: Verlag Bruno Hessling, 1970.

Tümpel 1971
Tümpel, Christian. "Ikonographische Beiträge zu Rembrandt. Zur Deutung und Interpretation einzelner Werke (II)." *Jahrbuch der Hamburger Kunstsammlungen* 16 (1971): 20–38.

Tümpel 1984
Tümpel, "Die Rezeption der Jüdischen Altertümer des Flavius Josephus in den holländischen Historiendarstellungen des 16. und 17. Jahrhunderts." In *Wort und Bild in der niederländischen Kunst und Literatur des 16. und 17. Jahrhunderts*, edited by Herman Vekeman and Justus Müller Hofstede. Erfstadt, Lukassen Verlag: 1984.

Tümpel 1986
Tümpel, Christian. *Rembrandt: Mythos und Methode*. Königstein im Taunus: Langewiesche, 1986.

Tümpel 2006
Tümpel, Christian. "Traditional and Groundbreaking: Rembrandt's Iconography." In Amsterdam/Berlin 2006.

Valentiner 1957
Valentiner, Wilhelm Reinhold. *Rembrandt and Spinoza: A Study of the Spiritual Conflicts in Seventeenth-Century Holland*. London: Phaidon Press, 1957.

Veldman 1999
Veldman, Ilja M. "Protestantism and the Arts: Sixteenth- and Seventeenth-Century Netherlands." In Finney 1999.

Veldman 2001
Veldman, Ilja M. *Profit and Pleasure: Print Books by Crispijn de Passe*. Rotterdam: Sound & Vision, 2001.

Verbeek 1992
Verbeek, Theo. *Descartes and the Dutch: Early Reactions to Cartesian Philosophy*. Carbondale and Edwardsville: Southern Illinois University Press, 1992.

Voss 1993
Voss, Stephen. *Essays on the Philosophy and Science of René Descartes*. Oxford: Oxford University Press, 1993.

Van de Waal 1954–55
Van de Waal, H. "Rembrandts Radierungen zur Piedra Gloriosa des Menasseh ben Israel." *Imprimatur* 12 (1954–55): 52–60.

Washington/Detroit/Amsterdam 1980
Blankert, Albert, et al. *Gods, Saints, and Heroes: Dutch Painting in the Age of Rembrandt*. Exh. cat. Washington, D.C. (National Gallery of Art), Detroit (Detroit Institute of Arts), and Amsterdam (Rijksmuseum), 1980.

Washington/Los Angeles 2005
Wheelock, Arthur, et al. *Rembrandt's Late Religious Portraits*. Exh. cat. Washington, D.C. (National Gallery of Art) and Los Angeles (J. Paul Getty Museum), 2005.

Weiss 2005
Weiss, Zeev. *The Sepphoris Synagogue: Deciphering an Ancient Message through Its Archaeological and Socio-Historical Contexts*. Jerusalem: Israel Exploration Society/Institute of Archaeology, The Hebrew University of Jerusalem, 2005.

Westermann 2000
Westermann, Mariët. *Rembrandt*. London: Phaidon Press, 2000.

Van de Wetering 2010
Van de Wetering, Ernst. *A Corpus of Rembrandt Paintings V: Small-Scale History Paintings*. New York: Springer, 2010.

Van de Wetering 2014
Van de Wetering, Ernst. *A Corpus of Rembrandt Paintings VI: A Complete Survey*. New York: Springer, 2014.

Wheelock 2005
Wheelock, Arthur. *Flemish Paintings of the Seventeenth Century: The Collections of the National Gallery of Art, Systematic Catalogue*. Washington: National Gallery of Art, 2005.

Winternitz 1977
Winternitz, Emanuel. "A Rabbi with Wings: Remarks on Rembrandt's Etching *Abraham Entertaining the Angels*." *Metropolitan Museum Journal* 12 (1977): 101–6.

Wittrock 1974
Wittrock, Irma. "Abraham's Calling: A Motif in Some Paintings by Pieter Lastman and Claes Moeyaert." *Konsthistorisk Tidskrift* 43, nos. 1–2 (1974): 8–19.

Yokohama/Fukuoka/Kyoto 1986–87
Brown, Christopher, et al. *Rembrandt and the Bible*. Exh. cat. Yokohama (Sogo Museum of Art), Fukuoka (Fukuoka Art Museum), and Kyoto (Kyoto National Museum of Modern Art), 1986–87.

Zachman 2007
Zachman, Randall C. *Image and Word in the Theology of John Calvin*. Notre Dame, Indiana: University of Notre Dame Press, 2007.

Zell 2002
Zell, Michael. *Reframing Rembrandt: Jews and the Christian Image in Seventeenth-Century Amsterdam*. Berkeley, Los Angeles, and London: University of California Press, 2002.

Index

Page numbers in *italics* refer to picture captions. All artworks are by Rembrandt unless otherwise stated.

Abraham
in the Old Testament 6–7, 11, 12, 16, 19–20, 23, 26, 27–28, 35–36, 41, 47, 51, 60
portrayed in art 16, 20–21, *21*, 28, *29*, *30*, 31, *32*, *34*, 54–55, *56*, 57, *57*, *58*, 59, *59* *see also under* Rembrandt
Abraham and Isaac *22*, 23–24, 41
Abraham and the Angels (mosaic, fifth century) 28, *30*
Abraham Caressing Isaac *6*, 24–26, *25*, 62n.15, 62n.16
Abraham Casting Out Hagar and Ishmael (drawing, 1650s) 62n.11
Abraham Casting Out Hagar and Ishmael (etching, 1637) *18*, 19, 21, 23, 26, 46, 47, 62n.10, 62n.11
Abraham Casting Out Hagar and Ishmael (Van Leyden) 20–21, *21*, 24
Abraham Entertaining the Angels (attrib. Bol) 55, *56*
Abraham Entertaining the Angels (attrib. Victors) 55, *56*, 64n.65
Abraham Entertaining the Angels (Bol) 55, *57*
Abraham Entertaining the Angels (copper plate, 1656) *43*, 45, 63n.48
Abraham Entertaining the Angels (De Gelder) 55, 57, *57*
Abraham Entertaining the Angels (etching, 1656) 12, *14*, 44, 47, *48*, 49, 54, 63n.52, 63n.57
Abraham Entertaining the Angels (Lastman) 28, *29*
Abraham Entertaining the Angels (painted panel, 1646) 6, 7, 11–12, *13*, 26–27, 31–36, *33*, *35*, *36*, 45, *46*, 47
Abraham Greeting the Lord and Two Angels (Muyckens) 31, *32*
Abraham Meeting the Lord and Two Angels (Bol) 59, *59*
Abraham on the Road to Canaan (Lastman) 32, *34*, 50
Abraham Prostrated before the Lord and the Two Angels (Maes, pen and ink drawing) 57, *58*, 59, 64n.67
Abraham Prostrated before the Lord and the Two Angels (Maes, red chalk drawing) 57, *58*, 59, 64n.67
Ascension 50
Augustine of Hippo 27–28, 31, 36

Bol, Ferdinand 6, 54–55, *56*, *57*, 59, *59*

Calvin, John 12, 19, 20, 29, 31, 32, 62n.29
Calvinism 12, 36, 42, 55, 60
and the portrayal of God 15, 32, 50, 63n.59
Cartesian philosophy 37, 42, 44, 60, 63n.34
Coornhert, Dirk 54
Cort, Cornelis *50*, 63n.60

Daniel's Vision of the Four Beasts 51, *51*, 63n.61
Descartes, René 37, 54, 63n.34
the divine portrayed
in art 15, 28–29, *29*, *30*, 31, 32, *32*, *34*, 50, *50*, 55, *56*, 57, *57*, *59*, 62n.23, 62n.29 *see also under* Rembrandt
in the Old Testament 6–7, 11, 12, 16, 20, 27–28, 29–31, 41
Dutch Reformed Church 62n.2 *see also* Calvinism
Dutch States Bible 19, 20, 31, 41, 42, 63n.40

Entombment 47, *47*

Felgenhauer, Paul 46
Four Men Seated under a Tree *42*, 44
Four Sufi Mystics (Mughal painting) *42*, 44, 45

Gelder, Aert de 55, *57*
Genesis 12, 16, 19–20, 21, 23, 29, 32, 50, 51
Chapter 18 11, 12, 15, 27–29, 44, 47, 51, 54–59
God Making His Covenant with Abraham 51, *52*, 54
God the Father Supported by Angels *53*, 54
Goeree, Willem 62n.28

Hagar *18*, 19, 20–21, *21*, 23, 62n.8
Heemskerck, Maarten van *50*, 51, 54

Isaac 23
birth 12, 19, 27, 28, 36, 47, 49, 51
portrayed in art *6*, *10*, 16, *17*, *22*, 23–26, *25*, 38, *39*, *40*, 41, 42, 62n.15
sacrifice 12, 16, *17*, 23–24, 38, *39*, *40*, 41, 60
Ishmael
as an allegory of the Jewish people 20, 45–46, 47, 63n.52
as ancestor of Mohammed 63n.46
destiny 20, 47, 49, 51, 63n.46
expulsion 12, *18*, 19–21, *21*, 23, 24, 46, 47
portrayed in art *18*, 19, 20–21, *21*, 23, 24, 46, 47, *48*, 49, 62n.11, 63n.49
Islam and Islamic art 44–45, 63n.46

Jacobsz, Lambert 62n.29
Jews and Judaism 12, 15, 20, 23, 27, 45–47, 51, 62n.10, 62n.23, 63n.52
Josephus, Flavius 23, 38, 41, 63n.46

Lastman, Pieter 21, 28, *29*, 32, *34*, 50
Leyden, Lucas van 20–21, *21*, 24
The Lord Commanding Noah to Build the Ark (Cort after Heemskerck) *50*, 63n.60
The Lord Commanding Noah to Build the Ark from the *Liber Genesis* (De Passe) 50, *50*, 63n.59

Maes, Nicolaes 57, *58*, 59, 64n.67
the material and immaterial in art 41, 42, 60
Menasseh ben Israel 46–47, 51, 63n.53, 63n.61
millenarianism 46, 47, 50, 63n.52
Mughal art *42*, 44–45
Muyckens, Jan Barentsz. 31, *32*

Old Testament 6, 12, 27–28, 29, 31 *see also* Genesis
optics in the seventeenth century 36, 37, 63n.34

Passe, Crispijn de, the Elder 50, *50*, 63n.59
Paul, the Apostle 20, 45–46, 60

Rembrandt van Rijn 6, 62n.2
pupils and followers 6, 54–55, 57, 59
works of art
anticipation in 19, 23, 24, 26, 29, 47
the divine portrayed 6–7, *10*, 12, *13*, *14*, 15, *17*, 29, 31–36, *35*, 38–45, *39*, *40*, *41*, *43*, *46*, *47*, 47–54, *48*, *51*, *52*, *53*, 57, 59, 60, 63n.42
illustrations for *Piedra gloriosa* 46–47, 51, *51*, 63n.53, 63n.61
material and immaterial in 41, 42, 60
motion and emotion in 15–16, 23–24, 38
portrayals of Abraham *6*, 6–7, *10*, 11–19, *13*, *14*, *17*, *18*, 21–27, *22*, *25*, 31–36, *36*, 37–44, *39*, *40*, *43*, 45–47, *46*, *48*, 51, *52*, 54, 59, 60
The Resurrection of Christ 16

Sacrifice of Isaac (drawing, ca. 1652–54) 38, *39*, 42
Sacrifice of Isaac (etching, ca. 1655) *10*, 38, *40*, 41, 42, 44, 60
Sacrifice of Isaac (painting, 1635) 16, *17*, 26, 36, 38
Sarah
in the Old Testament 11, 12, 19–20, 28, 51
portrayed in art *13*, *14*, *18*, 23, 27, 28, 34, 36, 45, *48*, 49, 51, 54, 55, 62n.10, 63n.49
St. Matthew and the Angel *41*, 42
St. Paul 60, *61*
Supper at Emmaus 32

Victors, Jan 55, *56*, 62n.29, 64n.65

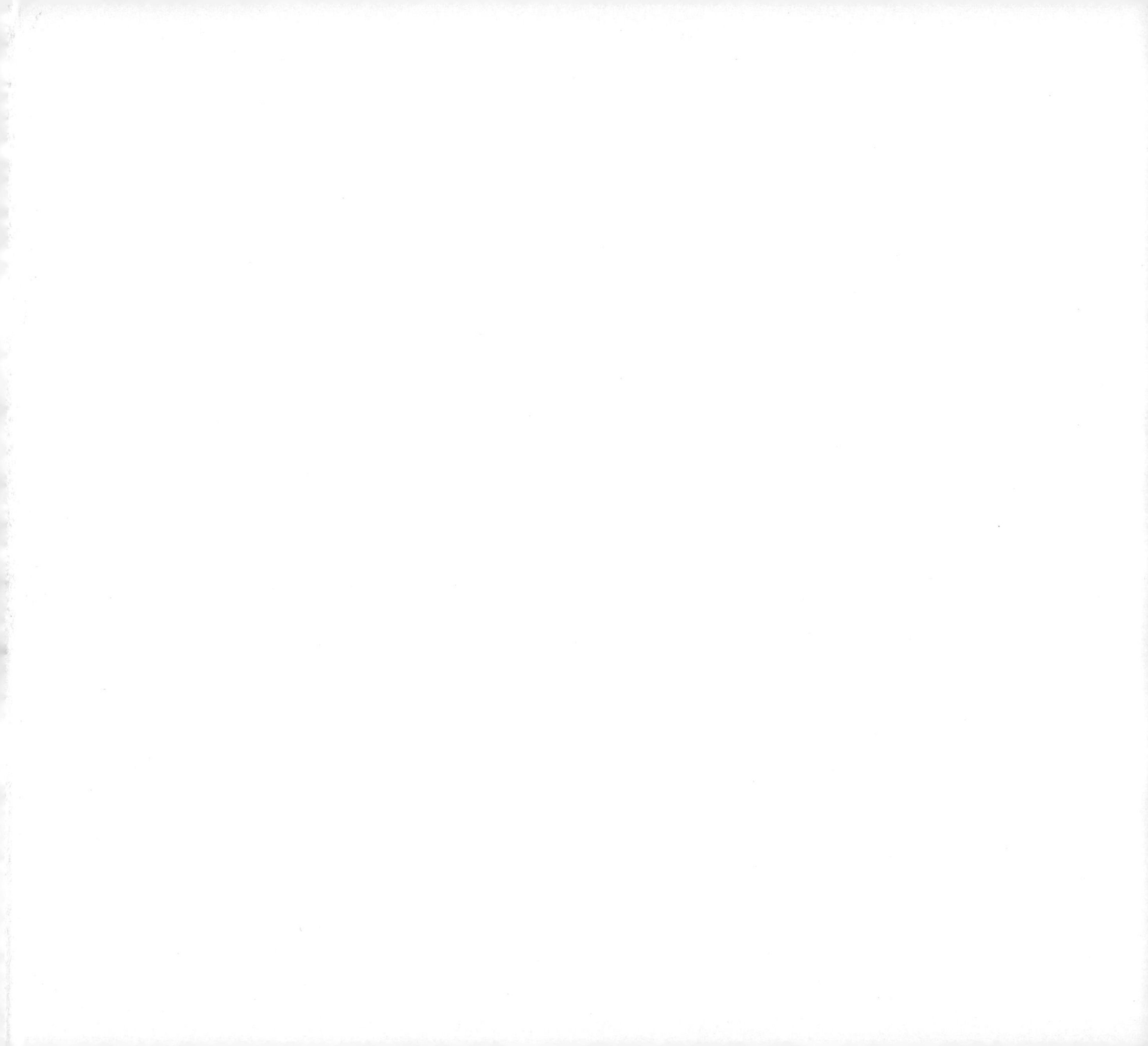